Good News of Great Joy

D0492270

Good News of Great Joy

Daily readings for Advent from around the world

Neil Paynter & Peter Millar

WILD GOOSE PUBLICATIONS

First published 2010 by
Wild Goose Publications,
4th Floor, Savoy House, 140 Sauchiehall St, Glasgow G2 3DH, UK.
Wild Goose Publications is the publishing division of the Iona Community.
Scottish Charity No. SC003794. Limited Company Reg. No. SC096243.
www.ionabooks.com

ISBN 978-1-84952-075-1

Cover image © istockphoto/seanshot

The publishers gratefully acknowledge the support of the Drummond Trust,
3 Pitt Terrace, Stirling FK8 2EY in producing this book.

A catalogue record for this book is available from the British Library.

Overseas distribution:
Australia: Willow Connection Pty Ltd, Unit 4A, 3-9 Kenneth Road,
Manly Vale, NSW 2093
New Zealand: Pleroma, Higginson Street, Otane 4170, Central Hawkes Bay
Canada: Novalis/Bayard Publishing & Distribution, 10 Lower Spadina Ave.,
Suite 400, Toronto, Ontario M5V 2Z2

Printed by Bell & Bain, Thornliebank, Glasgow

Contents

Introduction

In this book there are many inspiring words, so the introduction will be short!

A few months back, Neil Paynter and I were thinking about a Christmas book. Between us we came up with two basic ideas: one, that it should be a global book, and two, that each writer should reflect on the same words from the Gospel of Luke (Luke 2:10–11). This seemingly simple idea has come to fruition – thanks not only to all the contributors, but also to Neil's untiring efforts to contact and to encourage them.

It truly is a global book. Given the reality of our times, I do not think it's possible to read this book without being both humbled and inspired. It addresses both the heart and the mind. It takes us to new dimensions of the soul, and re-invigorates the compassion which lies deep in all of us.

Perhaps we can say that it is a book which celebrates life in all of its hopefulness, bewilderment and surprise. It carries a profound message of 'good news' and in doing that propels us to new levels of awareness.

I am sure that these pages not only will invite us to think more deeply about the central message of Christmas, but will also enlarge our understanding of this small planet on which we all share a common heartbeat, even if that fact is forgotten by many of us.

Peter Millar

But the angel said to them, 'Do not be afraid; for see – I am bringing you good news of great joy for all the people: to you is born this day in the city of David a Saviour, who is the Messiah, the Lord …'

Luke 2:10–11 (NRSV)

November 27

Luke 2:10–11

Children's voices round a campfire: Words from Uganda

I am writing this in Dar es Salaam – the Harbour of Peace – such a wonderful safe haven sheltered from all the storms and monsoons of the Indian Ocean.

I am afraid of disease – that terrible lack of ease, peace, good health – within our bodies and the bodies of those we care for and love. The moon is half full, rising above the ocean, with the evening star, Venus, dominating the otherwise black night sky.

'Don't be so scared!'

I remember a fragile young teenage girl in Uganda: Grace Bukenya. She was HIV-positive and on medication and doing well. One day in secondary school she died. Had she stopped her medication because children were laughing at her? I don't know. We, some school friends and colleagues from Elizabeth Glaser Pediatric AIDS Foundation, buried her in a little wooden coffin. I laid the only wreath on top. I looked over the tea and sugar plantations all around us and, though the day was warm, I shivered.

'Don't be so scared!'

The angels' voices are very faint.

I remember 40 HIV-positive boys and girls crying as the one-week Ariel

Children's Camp in Uganda came to an end. Now they must return to reality – hungry bellies, sarcastic aunties, ailing grandmothers. In camp we prayed for a cure for AIDS and always protection from evil.

'Don't be so scared.'

Over and over in scripture this simple message is truly a command.

The angels' voices are very faint.

Maybe this is because half of all of us in the Western world now spend half of our waking hours listening to other voices – television, mobile phones with internet access …

Some years ago my wife, Anne, and I spent a week in Iona Abbey during March – 'Cleaning week' it was called. I came across this 16th-century prayer from Frankfurt while browsing in the little Abbey library (a fabulous secret place!):

> *'Lord, teach me to silence my own heart that I may hear the gentle movement of the Holy Spirit within me and sense the depths which are of God.'*

The baby born in Bethlehem is somehow the opposite of fear. Jesus. God to the rescue.

God cares for us even in our weakest moment.

I remember round the campfire during each of the Ariel Children's Camps in Uganda when the kids started to share their deepest fears and uncertainties: 'Can an HIV-positive child really grow up and have a family?' … 'What if grannie dies?' … 'What will I do next week when I'm hungry?' Tears are wiped and we sit in silence staring at the dying embers of the fire. A few late sparks fly up into the blackest of skies. Then the children pray:

'Lord Jesus, be our Saviour and friend – the only help we have. Goodnight.'

Silence and trust and prayer. Over to you, God.

Salaam. Peace.

Willie Salmond

Willie Salmond is Regional Director of the Elizabeth Glaser Pediatric AIDS Foundation (www.pedaids.org). He is an Associate member of the Iona Community.

November 28

Luke 2:10–11

Around the world at Christmas

Astonishing words. And from an angel no less. And what I also find wonderfully comforting is that the angel was not speaking to the privileged and powerful, but to guys (and it would be guys in those days) tending their sheep on probably rather arid land, on the very margins of a great empire. The news was therefore announced to the hidden ones: to those who were making no claim to fame, but who knew that if they did not care for their sheep, life would be even tougher for themselves and their families.

And the message of extraordinary hope, which still resounds in human hearts, came to them during the night – in the stillness, when the world around them was quiet and only the stars illumined their fields.

This scene with the shepherds often came back to me when I worked in the villages of South India or in other poor parts of the world. And the revelatory nature of this encounter between the angel and the shepherds took on new meaning in these situations. For in these places of material poverty the word of the Lord is often much more profoundly understood than in places where affluence reigns.

It must be deep in the purposes of God, that the angel spoke of this great, good news – this earth-shattering news – to folk right on the margins of human society. And as I look back on my own spiritual journey which has taken me to many parts of our divided world, I believe that this particular relationship that God has with those at the edge is alive and well in our contemporary world. That in itself is for me fantastically 'good news' at a time when the lives of ordinary women, men and children in every continent seem to matter very little in the scheme of things to the powerful.

Of course the shepherds were fearful, as we would have been in such circumstances, but the angel's announcement also carries the astonishing tenderness of God. And that too is important in our times. For in every contemporary place of violence and of abandonment, the compassion and tenderness of God are also present. Go yourself to these places where the wounds of humanity are very great, and in the midst of it all there is moving a God who is himself or herself embedded in that mountain of suffering. At the heart of it, and many times also weeping.

And because that is true we must never romanticise this encounter between God's messenger and these shepherds of long ago. Of course it is an astonishing and surprising meeting, but for me it underlines God's limitless love of our human condition, and particularly in its ordinariness.

And it's at that point that the joy which the angel announced, and which was to be, amazingly, not for a select few but for ALL people, comes, so to speak, into its own. For it is the joy which comes from knowing that, however dark the night or however difficult the road, we are never abandoned by the One who sustains all. And my conviction is that today in our world, it is often those who have experienced deep sorrow and many wounds, who also know 'the joy of Jesus'. Paradoxical as it may seem, we see that reality at work time and time again. How can one not recognise it when a person riddled with AIDS and living in a leaking shack in a poor township in South Africa, says to you: 'You know, Peter, through it all one thing is true – the joy of the Lord is my strength.'

Around the world, at Christmas, these verses are today read in literally hundreds of languages. They are read in every country on earth, and the story of the angel and the shepherds is, as we all know, dramatised in a thousand ways. I love that annual returning liturgical journey to this wonderful narrative in Luke's Gospel. It is a narrative offering life, acceptance and hope to the modern mind – if we are open (as the hearts of the shepherds were) to receive it, and to be transformed by it.

Yet for me this remarkable story which has stood the test of time comes to life in that transforming way when I know, deep within me, that my heart is restless until it finds God. Up until that point, it is only a beautiful narrative, part of a familiar tale. It takes on *life* when I face the wounds in my own soul – and, in faith, believe that there is One who can heal and change me. A God who can re-make me, despite my seemingly endless inner contradictions, fears and hesitations.

This Christmas that angel still speaks to all of us who have ears to hear. And he or she is saying to us, as to the shepherds, a truth which is both powerful and tender, 'You *are* made in God's image, and you *are* befriended by Christ, and you *are* empowered by the Spirit.'

Prayer

Lord of every age,
help us today
to listen to the angel,
to reflect on the message,
and to be changed and made whole
each new day.

Peter Millar

Peter Millar is a member of the Iona Community who lives in Scotland. His books
include Waymarks: Signposts to Discovering God's Presence in the World; Finding
Hope Again: Journeying through Sorrow and Beyond; An Iona Prayer Book
(Canterbury Press); and Our Hearts Still Sing: Daily Readings *(Wild Goose Publica-*
tions). *Peter lived and worked in India for many years.*

November 29

Luke 2:10–11

The flare: One night in Yanoun

Crack – the flare exploded in mid-air, against the dark winter sky. A low-hanging green star travelled silently downwind, lighting the valley with a strange intensity, throwing harsh shadows from rocks and among olive groves. Why was it fired? What would happen next? We stood and gazed and shivered and wondered.

If it had been at home, in the West of Scotland, on our rocky coast, it would have meant a boat in trouble at sea. Folk would have heard it, watched it, knocked on neighbours' doors or rung round to find out if anyone knew what was happening, or who was missing. We have a coast-guard station on the Ross of Mull, but the nearest lifeboats are at Tobermory or Oban, several hours' journey away. So it would be a time of wondering, praying 'for those in peril on the sea'.

But last winter I was on the West Bank for three months, in the Occupied Palestinian Territories more than fifty miles from the Mediterranean. It wasn't a stormy night, but cold enough for frost, deep in the hills. It may have been a starry night, but we found it hard to see the stars' beauty because of security lights and spotlights glaring from settlement buildings on the hilltops. 'We' were a small international team of four, part of the Ecumenical Accompaniment Programme in Palestine and Israel (EAPPI) and based in the village of Yanoun as a 'protective presence'. For three months we shared the lives of the villagers, shepherds intimidated by armed men from the nearby Israeli settlement of Itamar, who wanted to drive away families who'd lived there for generations, to claim the land they farmed.

However, it wasn't settlers who had fired the flare, but soldiers from the Israeli army of occupation. We knew because we and our neighbours had seen their jeep arrive. We didn't know what this meant. Were the soldiers calling reinforcements to come and search the village? Would the men of the village be made to stand out in the street at gunpoint again? What did the soldiers suspect? Who were they searching for? Or was this support for the settlers who wanted the villagers to leave their homes? We and our neighbours were unarmed – we felt very vulnerable.

We went to the home of the village mayor, Rashed, and asked him what he knew and what we should do. He said 'Wait and watch', and invited us into his home. So we took it in turns to stand outside on the step, straining our eyes into the darkness and listening for other sounds, beside the village dogs barking, sheep bleating in the fold, the mountain wind. Standing outside made us visible in the spotlights – that was part of our reason for being there: to prevent violence not by being in any way threatening (which would have been hard!) but by making it clear that there were international witnesses to anything that happened in the village.

Meanwhile, the three accompaniers not on watch sat on mattresses and blankets on the concrete floor of Rashed's little house, with his and Wafa's six children, who snuggled close to their parents, first staring at us, then grinning, then giggling. In the middle of the floor was a charcoal brazier to keep us all warm. Wafa brought out strong sweet mint tea, and that warmed us up even more. And then – the children sat up and looked expectant – she brought in spoons and a steaming dish. In it was a wonderful pudding made with fresh milk from their sheep. Everyone had a helping (including the person keeping watch). We ate our fill. Wafa, their mother, knew that there are some things that can distract small children from soldiers and strange lights in the sky. In a way, it worked for us too.

The lookout called that the jeep had driven away. We saw its lights going up to the watch-tower on the hill above the village, and then disappearing. Rashed rang folk further down the valley, keeping track of the soldiers' movements. Then they had gone. This time nothing had happened – except intimidation. At last we went to our beds, though it took some time to sleep.

We had been afraid – and we had been accompanying people who were frightened with good reason. That night we experienced how God can be present and can drive away fear through community, down-to-earth courage and companionship – including a shared pudding.

Coming home to the West of Scotland, here is a prayer based on words attributed to St Columba, for folk on stormy seas, or amid political turmoil:

Christ, draw near to us, little people, trembling and most wretched,
rowing through the infinite storm of this age,
and bring us safely to the most beautiful haven of life. Amen

Jan Sutch Pickard

Jan Sutch Pickard was an Ecumenical Accompanier in the West Bank on two different occasions (www.eappi.org). She is a writer and storyteller living on Mull, a former Warden of Iona Abbey, and a member of the Iona Community.

November 30

Luke 2:10–11

'Do not be afraid ... see'

'Is there any hope for me?'
- A young man to his counsellor

'You told me my words were going to be secret ...... you frighten me again.'
- An asylum seeker in detention to those interviewing him

'I feel ugly inside and I hate myself ... I don't know how to live the rest of my life.'
- A convicted paedophile, living in the community on licence, to his counsellor

'I feel rubbish. I just don't want to do anything. I don't want to go on. I don't even want to go out any more. I'm scared.'
- A woman in mid-life, whose whole world has suddenly changed

Each of these people speaks from their own reality: the lived experience of fear. This common human experience can enter life at any time. And our reserves of hope can be sapped. Despair and fear take over. The effect of all this can be serious. A sense of isolation. No more safety and security. Feelings of inadequacy, loss of confidence and control, self-pity, anger, denial, feeling diminished, overwhelmed ...

To protect ourselves we can withdraw emotionally, physically and intellectually. Spiritually we can no longer 'see'. A sense of purpose, meaning, direction gives way to hopelessness ...

In a paradoxical way it is through the experience of there being no hope that a sense of hope can arise. In that recognition, something breaks in from outside and changes the experience. This is often through a relationship. Someone brings hope in … By attentiveness without judgement or criticism, or wanting to fix it, the fear may pass. There is more to the situation, yet to be experienced; the future may seem uncertain, but in a strange way feels secure, in the sense that, whatever happens, we will be able to face it and make something of it, even though we don't know what it will look like. Something makes sense, or we know meaning will come out of the situation, regardless of how the situation will turn out.

There is an ability to see beyond the present circumstances; an openness to new experience, to imagined, or unimagined, possibilities – living as if a new reality has already occurred, whilst struggling with present difficulties. There is a will to live, survive, recover or learn. A person can begin to 'see' again, or someone can 'see' for them, until they can see again for themselves:

'You are listening to me.'

'If you scare me I will run away, but you didn't scare me, you did something to cover me like. I can't explain it, it's just like you cover me with a wing and give me shelter inside … a warm shelter … makes me to express all my feelings.'

'I am more than I realised, more than my offences.'

'I think I'm beginning to accept it, even though I don't want to.'

For these people something has changed. Hope has entered their lives and they experience themselves differently.

Perhaps when life goes well, or is just predictably the same, we are less aware of hope. When difficulties or adversity comes then we become aware of the hope that is within us, or its lack. Hope is like food: once eaten it provides us with energy so we can function.

It is interesting that the message brought by the angels, a message of hope, is heard by the humble, the outcast, by those who are afraid. The message is that there is hope, and it is experienced through relationship. It is a call to move from destructive self-isolation into human relationship and community which is nurturing and sustaining. This offers the possibility of a restoration to wholeness and rescue from alienation from God, other people and oneself.

These words from the Gospel speak to people in the present reality of their lives. They are an invitation to 'see' life and their experience of it differently.

Hope can be so many things. It can pressure us into action: when others have no hope we can 'do' hope for them, with them.

Hope can also nourish, sustain and support us in situations in which no action is possible. Hope can help us live with a difficult present and an uncertain future; when we have to learn to wait for the moment when we can 'see' again and our fear subsides – transforming the experience of being scared into the sacred.

Prayer

God, help us to see those without hope and hold on to it for them until they are ready to experience it for themselves. Help us to renew our hope in your purpose and meaning for our lives and the life of the human family. Help us to see beyond present circumstances to your future for us.

John Prysor-Jones

John Prysor-Jones lives in a small village on the edge of Snowdonia in North Wales and works as a Specialist Psychotherapist in the NHS, and voluntarily for a counselling charity in Liverpool. He is an Associate member of the Iona Community.

December 1

Luke 2:10–11

'Do not be afraid': A checkpoint in Bethlehem, a funeral in Switzerland

When was I in desperate need of that message? In two different situations:

In 2007, I was an Ecumenical Accompanier in Bethlehem; one task was monitoring the large checkpoint Gilo. When we arrived at five in morning, there would be about 1000 men waiting in a long queue. They had to walk up through a narrow, wire gateway, which ended in an entrance the size of a normal door, leading to the first turnpike.

One morning the gateway broke and the men came from all sides to go through this door. They pushed one another. I was already standing near the turnpike, where I usually spent the first part of the time to find out if the soldiers had opened the checkpoint in time. When I saw the masses of men squeezing and pushing, I became terrified. The men just fell when they were through. One man could hardly breathe any more and was in pain. Probably he had broken some of his ribs. As I had no water, I gave him strong peppermint tablets, which I always have with me to keep me going.

There I found myself in front of the crowd, looking into the men's eyes, shouting: 'Please move back, form a row, stand in line, do not squeeze any more!' Many understood. Slowly they started moving back.

A miracle had happened: They formed a row, and one after the other came slowly forwards through the doorway to the turnpike and the first check of their identity cards.

The Spirit of God was within the crowd; the situation calmed down. I knew well that the men were in desperate need to move on, to queue for the security check, and again wait to have their work permits and their identity checked. I also knew they were afraid of missing their buses to work … and losing their jobs.

I spent at least an hour at the entrance of the checkpoint, managing the crowds; many among the men thanked me.

To go through this checkpoint early in the morning took three hours. Later in the day it was faster.

Looking back I imagine that more than one angel was present among the crowd, guarding them.

Two days later, I was again on duty. To my surprise the men stood quietly in a row. Some of them looked at me and nodded: 'You were right, thank you again.' As an elderly woman I was like a mother to these men. And a voice deep in me kept repeating: 'Do not be afraid, I am with you.' Was it the angel? Was it God's voice? …

Another experience:

I was afraid when doing the funeral of my best friend. She had asked me on her 80th birthday to be her pastoral carer, and to do her funeral – none of us expected her to die six months later.

She had been in intensive care for four weeks – she did not want to leave her world. She could not speak, but it was obvious that she was not ready to let go; she wanted to stay with her beloved ones and all the plans she still had. After another five weeks she finally died peacefully. My last words to her on my last visit were: 'God guard you and bless you.' She whispered: 'Also you' …

Her last words gave me courage to do her funeral. But what would I do with my emotions? There was no room for my tears. Then I realised that my dead friend had given me the energy to do that task with love and compassion for her family and her friends. My feelings became caring, rooted in and nourished by the hope of Christ.

A few days later I had to lead a second service in her village in the mountain area of Engadin, where she had lived and worked nearly all her life. It was a beautiful end-of-October afternoon. I blessed her house and our way to the cemetery. A large crowd walked behind the horses taking her urn to the old church outside the village, where her ashes were put to rest. This second service was even more difficult. *'Do not be afraid, your voice will not fail, fulfil your task.'* These words guided me to the church to lead the worship of remembrance, thanks and hope. I could do my task, treasuring her blessing deep within me. I felt held in God's presence among us.

Meditation and prayer

'Do not be afraid' the angel told the shepherds of Bethlehem in Beth Sahour below the city. He also gave that message to the desperate crowd at the checkpoint, not far from the place Jesus had been born.

He tells it to all people suffering under the Occupation in Palestine, giving them the hope of the newborn baby Jesus.

May this good news reach all the places of distress and death all over the world …

You, Jesus, you were born in a shelter in Bethlehem.
Today you and your parents can no longer travel
from Nazareth to Bethlehem.
There is a separation wall.
As Jew and citizen of Israel you are not allowed
to enter your hometown.

Jesus, you lived in a time of war and occupation –
you died in utter despair on a cross on Golgotha among criminals.
You die again and again with every woman, man or child being killed.
Jesus, you are with the tortured ones.

May the light of the angels shine on each of them;
may that light also shine on the torturers,
on the soldiers who have to kill,
and on their commanders.
May your light enlighten them
to find ways of reconciliation and peace.

Elisabeth Christa Miescher

Elisabeth Christa Miescher: 'I am a member of the Iona Community and a feminist theologian (my Ph.D in 2004 was on 'Rizpah's mourning as resistance'). In 2007 I was an Ecumenical Accompanier in Bethlehem (www.eappi.org). I will never give up hope for a just peace there and in all troubled regions of our world. I am a mother and grandmother.'

December 2

Luke 2:10–11

26th anniversary of the Bhopal gas disaster – still waiting for justice

A little after midnight, early on 3rd December, 1984, toxic gas leaked from the Union Carbide insecticide factory in Bhopal, central India, killing an estimated 8000 people.

> *But the angel said to them: 'Do not be afraid; for see – I am bringing you good news of great joy for all the people: to you is born this day in the city of David a saviour, who is Messiah, the Lord …'*

I am suspicious of anyone claiming to bring good news of great joy for all the people. All the people? It is a trick of the powerful to claim that something is good for all people, but which turns out to be good for themselves and those like them. The Green Revolution in the 1970s, in which high-yielding crops were introduced to India to feed all the people, turned out to be good for the big landowning farmers and the agrochemical companies. The poor are still hungry and many have suffered at the hands of the chemical industry on the way – none more than the people of Bhopal.

Angels are a useful literary device for delivering such a message, since they have the appearance of being classless: neither rich nor poor, floating timelessly above history (although not entirely, since the angel is clearly male). In the strongly class-divided society of first-century Palestine, how would the shepherds recognise the angel? Does he have the calloused hands of a worker or craftsman, the grubby hands of a retainer, or the smooth hands of the elite? On whose behalf does he speak of good news for 'all people'?

This is the third time that Luke has used the angel to present the tension between fear and joy. The first, to Zachariah, an elderly priest, whose infertile wife will give birth to John; the second, to Mary, a teenaged girl, pregnant with Jesus; and now the third, to shepherds, workers, to explain the significance of Jesus as Messiah. Fear and joy.

The people of Bhopal were visited by an anti-angel, who brought fear where there might have been joy. Many women who were pregnant then miscarried, their children stillborn or born deformed. Ever since, teenaged girls have suffered gynaecological irregularities. Workers and the elderly have been left destitute.

Fear was the emotion which the survivors recall from the night the gas leaked. As the panic spread, people fled in all directions; sleeping children were bundled up and pushed onto the backs of lorries going anywhere; women who would never leave home without a burqa, ran in their underclothes; quick decisions were made about whether to save babies first or the sick, whether to wait for those out late to return. Come daylight: the hospitals overflowing, the streets littered with the dead – people and livestock, the Muslims' goats, the Hindus' sacred cows – people searching for their children, their parents, their loved ones.

Today, 26 years later, great joy is still elusive. The people of Bhopal still await justice. For them, there has been no saviour. In 1989, Union Carbide 'settled' with the Indian government, without consultation with the survivors, for the equivalent of $500 per affected person: the value of Indian lives to the US corporation. Senior executives have avoided trial and the company chairman, Warren Anderson, now enjoys his retirement as the US refuses to extradite him. Dow Chemicals, who acquired Union Carbide in 2001, refuses to accept liability, whilst profiting from India's 'economic miracle', splashing corporate sponsorship around to disinfect its past. The Indian government doesn't want to discourage major investors by making them accountable for their crimes. This year saw the first convictions, of some managers of the Indian subsidiary company, on a minimal charge: far too little and targeting the wrong people.

Fear and joy. The survivors have had no joy but they have been fearless. For 26 years they have confronted multinational companies, government politicians, corporate lawyers and brutal police in their demands for justice: for adequate health care; economic rehabilitation and employment; access to clean, uncontaminated water; proper environmental remediation of the factory site; commensurate compensation; and to bring those responsible to account.

The anti-angel – the gas – was the messenger of fear and devastation. There was no evil in the gas, but rather in the economic decisions of the company. The gas leak was a direct result of cutting back on 'unprofitable' maintenance and safety features at a factory. The cause of death and destruction was the logic of putting profits before people.

There is no easy saviour, just as Jesus is no easy saviour. Bhopal survivors say that even if they got their demands, there would be no justice, no joy, if the same logic is putting others at risk. There are smaller Bhopals occurring throughout the world, wherever workers die or are made ill through exposure to hazards at work, wherever the ever-increasing cocktail of chemicals in the environment damages people's health, wherever children are made sick because it is cheaper to pollute the air with factories, roads, incinerators.

The most vulnerable – children, the elderly, pregnant women, marginal workers: to whom the angel announced great joy – are those most at risk of chemical hazards.

Bhopal is a negation of the saviour. In an exact reversal of the angel's speech, the 'great joy' which was promised by the Green Revolution was experienced by the poor of Bhopal as fear. It continues today: the poor are the acceptable price for that great joy of the rich: economic growth. This is the negation of the Messiah, the false messiah. On the contrary, the Messiah heralded in the angel's speech is the one in Mary's reflection: *'He has brought down rulers from their thrones but has lifted up the humble. He has filled the hungry with good things but has sent the rich away empty.'* That is how to recognise the Messiah, the one who comes to the young girl, the old man, the workers.

Allahu Akbar
The Muezzin calls the Muslims to prayer in Bhopal
God is Great
But still the people wait.
Hari Ram, the Hindus chant
and the people wait for justice.
A few ring bells and pray to Christ,
waiting.
Waiting for God.
Where on earth is he?

In the beginning:

The gas has cleared, day broken, Sunita coughs and, through stinging eyes, looks and looks for her children amongst the sick, for signs from survivors returning, amongst the dead.

Where is God? Why has he abandoned us?

She slumps, filthy, against the factory wall. A young boy brings her water, some cooked rice. The boy's mother, across the street, sitting in her burqa, encourages her to eat. It is the first time she's eaten food from a Muslim.

She goes to the boy's mother and they share their grief, all they have.

Where on earth is God?

One day, Samira goes looking. She speaks to her workmates. If God was here he'd give us wages enough to feed our children, he wouldn't let our bosses humiliate us. Let's form a union whilst we're waiting for God.

Three days into their hunger strike, two women hold hands, sitting under a tarpaulin in Delhi to which they had returned when released from police cells they'd been taken to for lying down in a shroud in front of the office of their enemies. Behind them the placard reads, in Hindi, Urdu and English: Bhopal still waits for Justice. Where is God?

Eurig Scandrett

Eurig Scandrett teaches Sociology at Queen Margaret University, Edinburgh and carries out research into environmental justice movements. He is coordinator of the Bhopal Survivors' Movement Study and edited Bhopal Survivors Speak: Emergent Voices from a People's Movement *(2009, Word Power Books). He is an educator and activist in environmental, peace, gender and trade union issues and lives with his partner in North Berwick. He is a member of the Iona Community.*

December 3

Luke 2:10–11

Jesus the maize seed: Christmas on the edge of a village in Malawi

Remove the images of Christmas I grew up with and to which the birth of the Christ child were attached for me – there will never be snow, lights on pine trees, the midnight magic, a jolly red Father Christmas to celebrate the turning of the sun in the northern hemisphere.

November and December here are the times of waiting for the rains, tension increasing as the heat builds up, anxiety when the rains are late in coming. For many years of living here at the edge of a village, I knew I could not celebrate the Incarnation in my heart until the rains had broken. 1991 was a very trying time, as the rains did not break until 5th January, 1992, and I could not find peace until they did. Rev John Mbiti wrote in the 1960s that in Africa we cannot plan beyond the next harvest because if the rains do not come, there will be no harvest, no life at all.

Remove, too, the trappings of imperialism to which the gospel message was so often attached. The Romans brought the gospel to my native England two centuries after it had already been taken to Ireland (unencumbered by doctrine) to be enculturated into the spirituality already practised by the Celts, who had been living there for many centuries. What if Frumentius had not stopped in Axum, Ethiopia in the early 300s, but had carried on further south in Africa? Would the gospel package have differed from that brought only 150 years ago by missionaries from Britain and Germany? In Malawi today Jesus is seen not so much as a sacrificial lamb who takes our sins away, but as a maize seed which, by being buried in the earth and dying, brings us new life – feeding us body and soul.

Contemplative Sisters here have long sown maize seeds in time for them to germinate by the beginning of Advent, and flower at Christmas. They watch the young plants grow throughout the four weeks of Advent.

Advent starts in my heart as the seeds of the *msangu* trees ripen (*Faiderbia albida,* or Apple-ring acacia). For many years we used to collect the curly seed pods to paint gold for our Christmas tree, but now explore new ways of propagating the seeds, and encourage young boys, wanting to earn their school fees, to grow the seedlings to share with everyone who wants to use a natural, fully balanced fertiliser on their maize gardens, as soon as the rains break.

At the birth of a baby in a village here, the grandmother traditionally carries the newborn to the entrance of the house and lifts them to the roof, where the priestess pours water on the roof edge so that some drops fall from the grass thatch on to the baby. This ritual integrates the baby into the tribe, the clan and the family, bringing great joy as life continues.

For over twenty years now the grandmothers, and grandfathers, too, have had an enormous role to play in the raising of these children, as the children's parents have often not survived, many dying of AIDS. They had to grow all the food alone before school feeding programmes developed. I used to watch an old watchman and his wife boil diluted cow's milk over three stones every day to feed their tiny grandchild.

So the fears throughout our society today – of the old people of these disease-ravaged communities; of the remaining economically-active breadwinners on whom huge financial burdens and the social pressures of the cities have been placed; and of the school-leavers who cannot find employment, and who see no other demand for their talents and energies but the huge task of taking over the care of the babies and young children – are met on this night. In the same words as a grandmother in a Lancashire village spoke to me, 50 years ago: 'They bring their luv with them, you know, Lass!'

Prayer

Creator of the cosmos,
your greatest gift to us is love,
that sacred reserve of energy
which came into our world as a baby,
born in poor circumstances, long ago, far away.
Lead us to seeing such births today, nearby,
as bringing again your love to our communities;
and help us to become, ourselves, gifts of your love
to those we meet today.

June Walker

June Walker has lived in Malawi for 50 years and is seen as the Mother of permaculture in her country (See Permaculture *magazine, Spring 2009). She is an Associate member of the Iona Community. She writes: 'At seven years old I decided I wanted to spend my life in Africa but, apart from being a missionary, did not know how to get there. So, later, I married a boy from school and came out in 1957 to live a fascinating life, spending the last 28 years as a housewife in the rural areas (like 85% of the women in Malawi). So was in just the right place at the right time to take up permaculture as it reached here to provide sustainable solutions for agriculture, nutrition and health in our village and the country.'*

December 4

Luke 2:10–11

Finding our own voice: Words from Australia

The New South Wales Christmas bush is quite unlike the 'holly and the ivy' of the northern hemisphere. It is a light-green bush with terminal sprays of white star-like flowers in the late spring of November, followed in December by beautiful, swollen postbox-red calyces.

Summer evenings at Christmas are warm and relaxed. Daylight-saving lengthens our leisure after days of heat and busyness. It is a time for sandals and short sleeves when warm breezes pour through the open doors of the house and neighbours chat as they walk their dogs or tidy up in the garden.

Socially, there is a hectic build-up to Christmas. End-of-year exams are a climax for students and parents. Summer holidays are just around the corner. It adds up to a happy hubbub – everyone saying: 'I must get this (or that) done before Christmas.' The city department stores join in the festivity as if the message of Christmas belongs to them, especially. It is 'good news' for them. There is a tacit agreement between church and commerce.

Handel's Messiah is heard on radio many times before Christmas. The soprano sings: *'And the angel said unto them: Fear not; for behold I bring you good tidings of great joy…'*

Yet 'fear' is not the first thing that comes to Australian minds before Christmas. The season of Advent is a happy time. The weeks leading up to

Christmas are often the best celebration of the Christ child's coming, more than Christmas Day itself. Carols are being practised, children think eagerly of presents, families come willingly to services. Perhaps there is a new baby born who can be laid in the crib when the Advent candles are lit for Mary's Sunday. Christianity and culture seem at ease with each other.

And might feel at ease if the religious voices of our culture really sounded true – as real and natural as the waratahs in the bush or the flannel flowers and heath flowers along our National Park track. It is still a challenge for us to find our distinctive voice for Christmas.

We listen, almost enviously, to Indigenous voices. David Mowaljarlai, in the far northwest of the land, brings us 'news' – everyday news that is a blessing:

> *You know … when daylight starts, it wakes me up. I can't sleep any more. It wakes the whole body. So turn round and have a look. There is brightness. Piccaninny daylight makes you feel like a different person. Morning gives you the flow of a new day – aah! …*

> *With this beautiful colour inside, the sun is coming up, with that flow that comes straight away in the morning. The colour comes towards me and the day is waiting …* *

Yorro Yorro, his book of writings, is filled with this natural peacefulness and goodwill, this love and acceptance of the world around him. It surprises us

---

* *From* Yorro Yorro: Aboriginal Creation and the Renewal of Nature: Rock Paintings and Stories from the Australian Kimberley, *Mowaljarlai, D. and Malnic, J., Magabala Books Aboriginal Corporation, Broome, Western Australia, 1993*

that Aboriginal spirituality and Celtic spirituality share so much. How simple and pure these voices seem, and it would be good if it were so simple.

But the angel's words 'Fear not!' are words that bring news that is not our media's 'news'. In newspapers, television and film there are earthquakes, floods, accidents, bomb blasts, wars: this is 'news'. There is grim fixation on death as 'news'. It is almost an ideology. Secular society perversely worships death, not birth. Fear, not 'Fear not'.

How good the news of the Child Jesus is, contesting for space in our hearts, minds and souls. The birth of a child, the love of the parents, hope for the future – all say 'Yes' to life. Symbolically and emotionally we are able to worship a different God.

Prayer

Encouraging God,
we give thanks for warmth and neighbourliness;
for the joy of singing the Good News at Christmastime;
for spring flowers and new babies
and for the treasures of Aboriginal spirituality
and Celtic spirituality
which we can share and make our own. Amen

Peggy Goldsmith

Peggy Goldsmith: 'I was fortunate as a girl to grow up as an Australian Congregation-
alist with a strong feeling for 'the priesthood of all believers'. My career has been as an
educator in English as a Second Language. A first visit to the Iona Community in 1994

led me to join the Wellspring Community in Australia, where I became national co-leader with Neil Holm (2001–2005). I am an active member of the Uniting Church in Australia and am deeply concerned with asylum seeker and refugee issues. I am passionate about caring for our environment.'

December 5

2:10 那天使對他們說：'不要懼怕、我報給你們大喜的信息、是關乎萬民的.

2:11 因今天在大衛的城裡、為你們生了救主、就是主基督'。

Good News from China: The Amity Foundation

As a warm-up activity in an Oral English class on 'Expressing Emotions', I asked my students to discuss with a partner the question: 'What are you afraid of?' Their feedback provided interesting insights into their fears and anxieties:

'I'm the only one in my family to go to college. I'm the first one in my village ever to go to college. So I'm frightened of letting everyone down.'

'If I don't pass the exams I'll never get a good job. I'm feeling a lot of stress. My parents work hard to find the money for my college fees.'

'I'm afraid about my parents' health. They're old. They shouldn't be farming any more. I help them as much as I can during the holidays but farming's hard work and they need the money for my tuition fees.'

Listening to these students struggling to express their fears made me wonder how the issues they raised could be or were being addressed, and has since led me to ask myself some questions:

What does 'good news' mean for millions of Chinese people who, in 2010, still live in relative poverty? What's the good news for subsistence farmers struggling to make a living and afraid that their children will be faced with a similar lifestyle, unless they find the money to give them an education? How can good news be spoken to college students afraid of failing exams and so fearful of ever being able to find a good job?

For the past three years I have been working as an English teacher in China. I work for the Amity Foundation, which in turn falls under the auspices of CTBI (Churches Together in Britain and Ireland) and BIATG (British & Irish Amity Teachers' Group). During this time I have witnessed how Amity is transforming people's lives by bringing the good news of 'love in action' to millions of people across this vast country.

The Amity Foundation was created in 1985 on the initiative of Chinese Christians, and everyone involved works to promote either education, social services, health or rural development for all Chinese people, regardless of religious affiliation (or none). During its early days, Amity concentrated its efforts in China's eastern coastal areas but gradually their work has moved westwards to where the needs are greatest, i.e. to the minority areas of western China: Guangxi Province in the south and Gansu Province and Inner Mongolia in the north.

The Amity Foundation stresses the need for co-operation, creativity, compassion, commitment, competence and communication. Using these six elements as a foundation, Amity's work demonstrates powerfully how good news can be (and is being) spoken to the fears of so many people in China and illustrates how good news is translated into action. The Amity Foundation is constantly searching to identify shifting local needs and, in doing so, to be creative in finding 'new ways to touch the hearts of all'.

In China, there are an estimated 40 million Christians, many of them speaking minority languages. Amity Printing, which is China's only authorised publisher of Bibles, is now the world's single biggest producer of Bibles. This joint venture between Amity and the United Bible Societies has been so successful that, to keep pace with demand, they have now moved into new premises on the eastern outskirts of Nanjing, where they have the capacity to print a million Bibles each month. In December 2007 the company printed their 50 millionth Bible and, of this total, 40 million were made available across China by a distribution system managed by the official church.

Amity's Educational Programme is based on co-operation between the sending agencies, the Amity Foundation and partner schools and colleges. Christian sending agencies across Europe and in America (in the UK, CTBI and BIATG) recruit and send English teachers to work in China to help improve oral English speaking skills, to raise more awareness of modern teaching methodologies and to help students and teachers acquire intercultural communication and awareness skills.

In its Educational Programme, Amity has introduced projects for the children of migrant workers and educational sponsorship for orphans. Its Young Volunteers' Programme recruits young people to come to China to spend a year teaching Oral English in middle schools. The Summer Tutoring Programme enables college students to return to their home villages to teach basic English skills to groups of primary/middle-school children, who maybe do not have the opportunity to go to school.

Another recent innovation in Amity's Educational Programme is '3-in-1'. In the future, Amity teachers will not only teach English skills to students; they will also work alongside Chinese English teachers in their college/university on programmes of Continuing Professional Development and will also hold training programmes for Middle School teachers in their area. Teachers in China are bound by an educational system which concentrates heavily on textbooks and examinations. It is hoped that this new programme will widen teachers' horizons, both educationally and culturally. In this way ripples of concern (the good news) radiate outwards to encompass even more people in Amity's circle of care.

Prayer

Loving God, we pray for the people of China, for Chinese Christians and for all who are connected in any way with the Amity Foundation.

Bring the good news of peace to students afraid and burdened by family expectations.

Bring the good news of hope to parents wanting a better life for their children.

We ask these things in the name of Jesus Christ our Lord, the One who comes among us, who tells us not to be afraid, who is Good News for all people. Amen

Kath Saltwell

Kath Saltwell is an Anglican priest and member of the Iona Community. Following a 3-year term of service in Uganda with VSO, she studied for her BD at Edinburgh University. Her theological training took place at Westcott House in Cambridge, where she also studied for a Master's degree. Since completing a 4-year curacy with the Worcester South East Team, she has been working as an English teacher for the Amity Foundation in China.

December 6

Luke 2:10–11

Listening for the sound of the Divine voice

In a society where fear is not only prevalent, but also preyed upon and increasingly stoked, the words 'do not be afraid' can easily fall upon closed ears. For a small number, the message will be heard as music to the ears, but for others, the message will simply travel in one ear and out the other. The directive 'do not be afraid' is not the only part of this message, and yet the remainder of the message has the potential to be completely lost, if the hearer looses interest after the first four words.

These words of truth, 'the Messiah has arrived on earth', are only heard as truth by those who are listening and looking for the truth. How many of us – realistically speaking – would have listened to the message if the angel had appeared to us? Or who of us would have listened if the message came from a different messenger … the minister on Sunday? … your best friend? … your mum?

Whether we would have listened then or now, we have the opportunity to contemplate the encounter because someone thought it should be written down for us. The message of the gospel in this encounter is still as true for us today as when it was written: I am bringing you good news of great joy for all the people. The Divine One has come to dwell on earth – in the still small quiet of the 'in between hours' of dusk and dawn, the Divine 'crept in beside us'.

Each week during the main part of the season on Iona, we are reminded every Saturday night in our evening liturgy of welcome that Jesus often comes to us in the guise of a stranger. The angel was like a stranger to the shepherds; but our society doesn't have much 'space' for receiving the stranger – let alone the angel who has come to cast out our fears and to speak a great truth.

The good news is for ALL the people.

The Divine does not discriminate from within the creation or humanity who is a recipient of the message or even whom the message affects. The message is the same regardless of skin colour, age, gender, level of education, status in society, amount of chlorophyll, number of legs, chemical composition, type of wings or lack of them, etc.

This message is for ALL the creation! This good news of the Word and Breath of God arriving as the Messiah in the form of a babe is for every part of the universe! Why? The Divine One loves all that has been created. The Incarnation shows us the fullness of this Divine Love coming in the form of a vulnerable, helpless babe – God's big risk – so that we can be released from the fear that holds us captive. The Kingdom of God has a different way, vision and truth. The currency in this Kingdom is Love!

So why has the Divine crept in beside us in the gentle hush of the silence of midnight to tell us this all-important news? Why the Divine in human form?

Perhaps one answer is to show us that the fabric of the universe is woven with strings of love. Perhaps another answer is because for the creation, to love is like breathing, it is part of our very essence and nature. Perhaps another answer is because God is love, and where God is, love is. Usually the birth of a baby comes from an act of love, and thus the baby is a conception of love in action; a means of giving more love and of placing more opportunities for love in the world. The propagation of love in action connects us to each other. Without love, and actively choosing love, we become overwrought with fear and anxiety, which leads us to the calamities of our world as we each vie for position, prominence and prosperity at the cost of others and the creation.

The writer of 1 John 4 says: 'With Love there is no room for fear; indeed perfect love banishes fear. For fear has to do with punishment, and anyone who is afraid has not attained to love in its perfection.' (1 John 4:18, Revised English Bible).

This is good news. But how do we see it? How do we hear it?

The Divine comes in human form in the wee hours of the night, and does anybody hear? Look at our world, rife with fear, anxiety, jealousy, war, injustice … how will they hear? The story of Elijah on Mount Horeb (1 Kings 19) gives me courage for our world, not just myself: that in Elijah's desire and persistence, he waits through the wind, earthquake and fire – until there is nothing left but the sheer silence. Then, in the sheer silence, Elijah hears God's voice speak to him.

Until the people of God reclaim the importance of silence, stillness, solitude, and listening for the sound of the Divine voice, we cannot impress upon our world this need either. And until then, our world will continue on its trajectory to destruction with a people who have not heard the Good

News – the good news which is for ALL: 'do not be afraid'; perfect love is part of the fabric of the world.

What is one way that you can actively reclaim the importance of silence, stillness, solitude and listening for the sound of the Divine voice this Advent/Christmas season? How might this change in your life, affect the lives of those around you? How can you show the Good News that perfect love casts out all fear?

Prayer

Breath of God, breathe upon us that the feel of your exhalation may raise the hairs on our necks and cause our ears to prick up at the sound of your voice. May we hear fully your message of truth for all creation and be inspired to live out this truth in the everyday of our lives and know intimately its freedom. Help us to be agents of your Perfect Love, living in freedom from fear. Amen

Jamie Schmeling

Jamie Schmeling is a minister of the Reformed Church in America and the Deputy Warden on Iona.

December 7

Luke 2:10–11

A wellspring at the bottom of our existence: Words from Sweden

'Good news of great joy'. These are the words that caught my attention in this text. I believe that, in a world where cynicism, indifference and control are considered cool attitudes, to cultivate a counter-culture of joy could be a strong statement for the engaged life.

Joy in this sense is not a superficial, happy-clappy expression of a faith that shies away from the fact that life is sometimes difficult, even for Christian people. It is the joy that seems to lie at the bottom of all spiritual experiences, as they are recorded by the great mystics. An intense joy in the midst of, and in spite of, an equally intense awareness of suffering.

The Swedish poet and Salvationist Majken Johansson talks about the 'bottom joy' in one of her poems. She suffered from severe depression and alcoholism all through her life, even as she was an engaged Salvation Army soldier. She did not hesitate to share her angst as well as her joy in her poetry. When she writes about 'bottom joy' it is in the double sense of bottom as the ground of existence and as the depth of depression:

From thousand and one anxieties
I am liberated.
The bottom joy
Is sufficient for all bottom situations.
(My translation)

Joy as an antidote to anxiety – or joy as the result of liberation from anxiety. Maybe it works both ways? The connection is clear from the angel's message to the shepherds: *'Do not be afraid; for see I am bringing you good news of great joy.'* Fear can prevent us from experiencing joy, but once we have found the 'bottom joy' we have found a way of diminishing fear.

The shepherds were at the bottom of society. It was probably not because they were overly pious that the angel approached them. Maybe it was just because they happened to be there – out in the night, while wealthy and established people were asleep in their houses. And maybe they were still a bit fearful, probably their immediate feeling was not joy, but they were sufficiently curious to follow the angels.

Swedish author Selma Lagerlöf has written a legend about one of the shepherds – a grumpy and rather repulsive character. He is approached by a man who we will understand is Joseph, but throws his staff at him to chase him away. But he is astounded to see that the staff is caught halfway in the air. This makes him curious, and he follows the man, becoming increasingly intrigued when he finds that wild animals don't harm him, and that he can gather burning coals in his cloak without being burnt.

He follows the man to a cave where a woman with a child is waiting, the child shivering with cold. As he sees this, his heart is moved, and he offers the child a sheepskin. In that moment, his eyes are opened and he can see that there are angels all around, and that they have protected the man from being harmed by the fire and the wild animals. And his heart is filled with joy.

Selma Lagerlöf concludes her story, which is told by a grandmother to her granddaughter: *'You see, it is not about lamps or lights, but about having eyes that can see the glory of the Lord.'* And, the story tells us, these eyes are the eyes of compassion: when we are no longer afraid of the stranger but meet him with curiosity and empathy.

The Gospel invites us to find joy as a wellspring at the bottom of our existence, in the dark depths in our own lives and in extending empathy to others who are at the bottom.

Prayer

God, Source of all joy,
make us brave in the face of fear,
joyful in the face of cynicism and
compassionate in the face of indifference.
Amen

Helene Egnell

Helene Egnell: 'I live in Stockholm and am an ordained minister in the Church of Sweden, currently working as Bishop's Adviser at the Centre for Interfaith Dialogue in the diocese of Stockholm. I am an Associate member of the Iona Community and active in the Iona-inspired network in Sweden.' www.iona.brommadialogen.se/index.html

December 8

Luke 2:10–11

Good News of great joy to humanity: Words from Kenya

From the word go, God intends that the human race has something more than gold. Thus the end result was for humanity to realise divine peace, which would only come to pass through God's paternal relationship to Jesus Christ. In essence this would also mean God's fatherly relationship to his creation, but more so to believers as his children.

We believe that Jesus came to be with us through a miracle: The Lord of Heaven and Earth came into human flesh and nature and, though from eternity, true God now was also sinless man. This one person stood as both God and Man between God and humanity. He represented sinful humanity before God, and the just and loving God before humanity.

The birth of Jesus Christ is the foundation of understanding and experiencing God's heart.

God's ultimate provision of peace is evident in the person and works of Jesus Christ. It is only through Christ that peace with God can be achieved and maintained. Peace would lead to a state of delight and happiness which is grounded in the work of God the Father, Son and Holy Spirit. Joy is experienced in many circumstances of human life; but it is essentially expressed in the life of God's people who experience joy in response to all that God has done for them.

The world today is corrupt, the corruption spreading like a dense fog throughout society. It is even spread by those who are safe, ordinary, dull and anti-social. God's work of salvation may be seen as an accomplishment of Jesus Christ through the cross and resurrection. By faith, the believer is capable of sharing in the saving benefits won by Jesus Christ. But this calls for humanity to embrace a life of dependence upon God in the name of Jesus Christ – may the dear believing folk be a bright reality of fulfilment of Christ's calling and live as witnesses to him through the power of the Holy Ghost.

The chief characteristic and fundamental doctrine of the Gospel is that Jesus Christ is both Lord and Saviour. Initially, God made a covenant with Adam and Eve in paradise and promised to be their daily companion, and in return, they promised to obey him; but they disobeyed and broke the covenant. However, that didn't change God's decision to be a covenant God. God chose Abraham to be a father of a new community of people. With Abraham and his children, God made a covenant of grace unto ever-lasting salvation. Today, all believers in Jesus Christ are children of Abraham and members of God's covenant family.

To all who believe and submit to its demands, the promises of the Gospel include forgiveness of sins, new life in Jesus Christ and adoption into the family of God.

As Christians, we confess that we belong to Jesus Christ and want to be his followers. We like to think of ourselves as a family. We live under the authority, love and care of a father to whom we must give childlike trust and obedience. Sometimes, our characters may make us seem aloof to others, and sometimes we have family squabbles in the political and work environment. But may the Lord God help us to emulate that perfect relationship in Jesus Christ – unity in diversity: to be able to weep with those who sorrow, rejoice with those who celebrate, bear each other's burdens, increase each other's joy and enrich each other's lives. Amen

Prayer

Shepherds on nightwatch are blessed by a vision; and indeed are so terrified by the impact of the miraculous light. Not realising that the Lord of Heaven and Earth had come into human flesh and nature.

Lord, for those forced to leave home on a journey due to one thing or another, grant them journey mercies in whatever they must endure. Lord, hear our prayer.

Marksen W. Masinde

Rev. Marksen W. Masinde: 'I am Moderator of the Kenya Christian Reformed Church, and the Director of Trans Nzoia Teachers Training College for primary teachers situated in Kitale town. I have once contested for a parliamentary seat in Lugari constituency and look forward to contesting the same in the year 2012. I have six children and live in the western part of Kenya. I am an Associate member of the Iona Community.'

December 9

Luke 2:10–11

Six simple words

'To you is born this day'. Six simple words at the centre of the angel's proclamation have caught my attention. So simple, these words could be said to any new parent. A new son, a new daughter is born to a family which will receive the bundle of joy, embracing the life, the energy, the mess and the marvel of a baby. The gift that is Christ is handed to us in these simple words which could mark the beginning of our relationship with any newborn.

Of course, it isn't just any newborn at the centre of this text. The angel had done some homework. This message is cast in the language the Roman assembly had used to celebrate the birthday of Caesar Augustus. Yes, the Romans had greeted 'the most divine Caesar' with 'good tidings' 'for the whole world'. Romans called Caesar 'a saviour who put an end to war', 'born for the common benefit of all'. The angel gives the newborn in the city of David a birth announcement to rival the emperor. And then the angel wraps this child in the expectations of God's people. The child which the angels proclaim will be the Messiah, anointed with the people's hopes and God's promise of joy, joy that will rearrange the claims of Caesar and replace peace maintained by Roman swords with peace that puts an end to fear.

I found these historical quotations about Caesar in my research for a Bible study on Luke which I lead in my parish each week.* When I read the citations aloud in our group, jaws dropped. How could the beautiful poetry of the angel's message echo the self-serving praise of an emperor who called himself divine? It was a good reminder that Jesus was born into a moment similar to ours – with posturing politicians, precarious loyalties, tensions among God's people about how the future will unfold. The angel's message wasn't written on a greeting card. It rang into a world where God's people had to make a choice. Would they take their peace as Caesar served it up, keeping within the structures he had established – mostly to ensure his own power and prominence? Or would God's people embrace this newborn and receive a Saviour who would call them to respond, sharing great joy with all people in ways they hadn't yet imagined?

'To you is born this day'. Six simple words which contain a profound challenge for us as they ring out amid the structures of a world in which ruling powers serve the interest of too few. These six simple words ask us to receive God's promise of hope as it comes to us in the newborn Christ and then do something about raising that hope in our generation. I need to hear the challenge in the angel's message these days. I find this moment one in which people in Canada have surrendered responsibility to act in hope in and for our communities. We expect good things to be delivered to us by those in power yet we seem unable to recognise the self-serving interests in our leaders who say one thing and do another. Not unlike Caesar Augustus.

The angel delivered a wake-up call in our Bible study group. When we reach out to cradle the One who is born to us, we receive God's gift. We also receive the responsibility to do our part in facing the powers around us with a new and different vision of great joy for all people. 'To you is born this day'. Six simple words which anoint us with the hope and joy of God's gift of new life. Our challenge – to act in hope and joy so that God's gift takes flesh over and over again to change the world God's way, not Caesar's.

Prayer

God of power and new possibility, you place your gift of joy and hope into our arms as we cradle the Christ child once more. Wake us up to our responsibility to receive the joy that is born to us in him. Anoint us with hope to live out the new possibilities you create for all people through our Saviour and Lord. Amen

Nancy Cocks

Nancy Cocks serves as minister of St John's Presbyterian Church, Medicine Hat, Alberta in Canada. She is a former Warden of the MacLeod Centre on Iona, and the author of Growing Up with God: Using Stories to Explore a Child's Faith and Life; *and* Invisible We See You: Tracing Celtic Threads through Christian Community (*Wild Goose Publications*). *She is an Associate member of the Iona Community.*

*The quotations from Roman historians are cited in The Gospel of Luke: The New International Commentary on the New Testament, *by Joel B. Green, W.B. Eerdmans Publishing Co. 1997, p.133.*

December 10

Luke 2:10–11

God is not emperor!

What was God *really* saying when the angels appeared to the shepherds in the middle of the night? Clearly the message is deeper than the much repeated 'good news of great joy'. And why are shepherds the first to hear this message? Christmas still today lifts up in me so many questions, and this is the challenge – to seek for answers to these questions at this time in history; this is what makes Christmas so incredible to me!

I am sure that when the angels said 'do not be afraid' they chose these words because so many people at the time were living in fear. In a world in which, like today, there were so many women, children, men, young and old people living in fear, these were very meaningful words: 'Don't be afraid.'

When Jesus was born, the all-powerful emperor ruled most of the world. The census for which Joseph and Mary had to travel was a manifestation of this power: how many people could be taxed? How much could they be taxed to pay for the megalomaniacal dreams of the emperor? How many young men could be drafted into the armed forces?

People lived in fear that they would be sent to fight other people's wars in distant lands, people were afraid of how much money would be taken from them, people were afraid that even their basic dreams would be shattered – how to keep the family in the dignity God has talked about through the prophets: build your house and live in it, plant your vineyard and enjoy its fruits, enjoy your children and old age sitting under the fig tree (Mic 4:4)? People felt these were their basic rights, yet they lived in fear the emperor would not allow this.

So on that night when the shepherds were out in the fields, caring for animals which most probably were not theirs in the first place, and God wanted the people to know about the amazing event that had happened and rejoice, God knew that the first words people heard were crucial; this is why the angels said *'Don't be afraid'*. This marked the whole difference: while the emperor was to be feared, God was not. While the emperor represented pain and death, God was present as Life and Hope. While the emperor reminded them of Pharaoh and the cries of the people, God was Liberation and Exodus.

The Good News was Salvation. The Messiah was no longer the 'expected one', the Messiah was now real. Things were going to change for the better: God took on a human form, reminding us, once again, that to God, humanity is something to be valued, not despised. And the human form that God chose was that of a baby, reminding us that God was choosing a shape most people rejected (this would happen again on the cross).

And all this happened to shepherds, sleeping out in the cold of the night, as so many people in this world do, night after night. To people who find little to enjoy in life, God speaks words of joy, of hope, of transformation, of life. From the very beginning of this event, God questions the current situation of the times we live in, based on power, on economic injustice, on destruction of the earth.

God is not emperor! The message of hope questions all structures which condemn people to live in fear, people who sleep out at night, be it in Bethlehem, Buenos Aires, Rio de Janeiro, Port-au-Prince, Jerusalem, London, Accra, Mumbai or any other place on earth. God's message continues to bring down fear, to present hope as the central issue of this transforming action in history.

The Saviour is real, is fragile, is persecuted, is transforming life, and is questioning all exercise of power which does not allow God's creation to rejoice and hope – this is why Christmas and Easter are so connected; manger and cross are symbols of power's dehumanisation and of God's option for new life.

Christmas once again questions:

– our set ways
– our romantic vision of life: our happiness which condemns other people to live in fear
– our rejection of change

Christmas once again challenges us to:

– live in hope
– live in solidarity
– work for peace
– believe life in fullness for all must be the agenda

Prayer

Dear God, challenge us all – once again so that when we hear you speak of hope, of salvation, of new life, of new possibilities, we may realise you speak from the centre of life itself, and that you continue to want us to be part of the life-transforming story.

To all who live in fear, to all who have nowhere to turn to, to all who feel chased away, and to those who feel Christmas is only a shopping event, speak once more: 'Fear not, the good news is joy, is sharing, and is happening once again with you!' Amen

Robert H. Jordan

Robert H. Jordan was born in Argentina and lived and worked there for much of his life. He recently became a minister of the United Reformed Church, serving two congregations in England: Immanuel-Swindon, and Highworth. He is an Associate member of the Iona Community.

December 11

Luke 2:10–11

Looking for signs of joy and hope to share: A message from Brazil

As I begin this message, it is still winter here in Brazil, which means rain for most of the North and Northeast regions of the country. Having been stuck in bed with dengue for almost three weeks, slowly I begin to recover and take the risk of going for a walk by the sea. The picture before my eyes is beyond description: pieces of thousands of destroyed little homes brought by the river waters! Due to dreadful floods hitting over fifty towns from two states just a short drive from where I am living and working now, as a missionary.

I keep walking along the seafront, and three pictures stick in my mind: of those who bitterly complain about so much 'rubbish' on one of the beaches we are most proud of; of those who are eagerly trying to clean it as quickly as possible to pretend that nothing has happened; of those who, believe it or not, look for jewellery and other valuables on the sand and under the rocks … And what about me? I am tempted to feel fearful, hopeless and helpless … Deep down I share the pain of those harmed and invaded by nature. Suddenly reminded of my role in my new ministerial placement – to serve pastoral ministers and leaders, by training, equipping and support-ing them as they support their own flock – I simply ask: 'How?!'

Yes, I can join in the essential work of fellow volunteers and send water, food and clothes. I can mobilise leaders, churches and friends and encour-age them to do the same, but I also look for signs of joy and hope to share … Luke 2:10–11 then echoes in my mind: *But the angel said to them (the shepherds): 'Do not be afraid. I bring you good news of great joy that will be for all the people. Today, in the town of David, a Saviour has been born to you; he is Christ, the Lord.'*

As we approach Christmas and are challenged to reflect more and more on unexpected and difficult circumstances like this – both around us and in the world – what lessons can we learn from such a powerful statement?

- *'Do not be afraid':*

Fear seems to be innate to humankind as a way of self-protection; in this text, the shepherds, as much as most of us probably would, certainly feel uncomfortable with the angel's supernatural visit. Apart from their usual fears, they had to deal with this unexpected being, who surely disrupted their routine. And I wonder: Were they 'allowed' to be afraid, if they themselves were to provide care and security for their sheep? And further: why do we, sometimes, fear what comes from God, but are not necessarily afraid to expose ourselves to what is 'ungodly'?

Nowadays – perhaps more than ever – we fear loneliness, neglect, rejection, violence, death, the political system and most politicians, not having enough to survive on, and what is still to come … But isn't this extreme fear caused by our own self-reliance, lack of faith or not being familiar with God's agenda?

- *'I bring you good news of great joy':*

The angel calms the shepherds down; and reminds them – and us – of our vulnerability, no matter how safe we claim to be or what status we hold in society. We are all exposed: to political disagreements, economic crises, family problems, 'unexpected visitors', be they the effects of climate change, natural catastrophes or something else that causes fears, sorrows, concerns. However, in the middle of this chaos, there must be always someone bringing good news and there is certainly something good that is still worth being shared and can unbelievably bring great joy: the fact that a Saviour, a rescuer, someone who really cares for us has been born to us! Now, are we prepared to play the angel's role and be bearers of this good news, especially in times of trials and despair?

- *'for all the people'*:

Fear of rejection or loneliness is addressed here. There is nothing worse than feeling excluded and inadequate, so the angel's statement is a great reminder of the kingdom's inclusiveness: Jesus related most of the time with very ordinary people, and not exclusively with the high and mighty, as many of us have been seeking to do lately. If we are aware that his ministry was so focussed on the *'broken-hearted, poor, prisoners, blind and oppressed'* (Luke 4:18), why do we find it so hard to follow in his footsteps?

- *'Today ... a Saviour has been born to you; he is Christ, the Lord'*:

It is amazing not only to see the way that Micah's prophecy had been fulfilled (Mic 5:2), but also to marvel at how Jesus's full identity is summed up and provided in this portion of Scripture. He is identified not as an ordinary baby being born – but as Saviour, Christ and Lord. The angel leaves no space for doubts about this aspect! As Saviour, *'He came to seek and save what was lost'* (Luke 19:10); as Christ (the Greek word for Messiah, which is the Hebrew for 'Anointed one') he is meant to *'comfort all who mourn, and provide for those who grieve ... oil of gladness instead of mourning and a garment of praise instead of a spirit of despair'* (Is 61:3); as the Lord – Yahweh or God – his role is to be our 'owner' to have exclusive Lordship over us. Can we personally recognise him as such as we go through these lines of Scripture and approach Christmas? Or has Christmas become something else to us completely?

Prayer

Heavenly Father, thank you for sending Jesus to live among us, die on a cross in our place, as a perfect reminder of your love for us, and rise again. Deliver us from any fear of not being comfortable with your presence or your message and help us to understand the good news of great joy and to spread the fragrance of this oil of gladness to all the people, regardless of origin, gender, age or social class. May we never deny your full identity – and guide us all the way to the very end of our days! Amen

Léa Guimarães da Silva

Léa Guimarães da Silva, from Brazil, is an ex-Sheffield University student, as well as a former Iona volunteer, who has been back in her country for the last 10 years, working in education, pastoral care and community development, mostly among deprived and excluded people. She lives in the Northeast of Brazil and serves pastors and leaders, by training, supporting and encouraging them to make a difference wherever they are so that God's kingdom can be expanded. (www.sepal.org/brasil/english.htm)

December 12

Luke 2:10–11

Chosen to be his hands, his feet, his voice

The shepherds were paralysed with fear. Solid ordinary men doing an honest job, not considering themselves important. Down-to-earth, salt-of-the-earth fellows; no hoity-toity yuppie 'I am better than you' thoughts in their heads. The experience was mind-blowing. The music that exploded in the night from a choir in the heavens. Wow! And an angel telling them something important. They talked it over – they just had to go and see for themselves and experience what had been promised to them.

They left running as fast they could, eyes wide open; excited, falling down as they rushed to see this incredible baby, who was to be the Messiah. They saw and believed and went on their way and joyfully told everyone they came into contact with what God had revealed to them. The people were very impressed with their stories, and the shepherds reveled in the glory of all that they had experienced, knowing that their lives would never be the same again. A shepherd maybe, but a very special person to have had this message given to them. They pondered all of this in their hearts as they worked with the sheep. This was no dream, this was real and they had been chosen.

I reflect on what my reaction might have been … perhaps a cynical 'I don't believe you' and 'what is all that racket'? Too much bother to go and look for myself: let someone else see and affirm and then I'll go later. Or perhaps my curiosity would have compelled me to explore, to experience something new …?

I long to be chosen to experience the birth of new opportunities, new experiences that will lead me into a deeper understanding of who I was created to be. I am sure the shepherds held themselves in high esteem after their experience. We who hold on to negative thoughts about how good we are, need to know that we too were chosen to see this child. That he came so that we can see ourselves differently. We are special, chosen and included in all that he came into the world to do; and we are now his hands, his feet, his voice. We who feel as vulnerable as a baby at times are called to be nurtured by the words that flowed from his mouth, to enable us to grow into the people we were meant to be. To have courage, as the shepherds did, to tell those who feel unloved, lost in the desert, confused, that something special has happened and that things will never be the same again. That there can be a new beginning in our life and that the events of that night were not just for a few but for everyone, and that the best is yet to come …

Prayer

Dear Lord of new beginnings, help us to have courage as you ask us to trust you. To trust in something small that will grow into a lifetime of purpose. Help us to find our place in the world to which we have been called.

Lord, let us be your hands, your voice, your feet, whether we walk on the hot earth of Africa or the cold snows in Scotland. Help us, through community, to reach out to your people.

May your love surround and strengthen us and all with whom we come into contact, and may we reveal the glorious message that exploded in the skies to the shepherds to those who will hear us, and let them know that the best is yet to come. Amen

Muriel Connell

Muriel Connell is a wife, mother, grandmother, writer, storyteller and traveller. She left Glasgow in l974, and now lives in Strand near Cape Town, South Africa. She has written two booklets: Life Journeys: The Road to Wholeness, *and* Discovering Diamonds in the Desert *(www.lifejourneys.co.za). She was a member of the Iona Community's Resident Group on Iona in 2003.*

December 13

Luke 2:10–11

Outstretched hands

We are in the Basilica of St Francis, in 'his' town, Assisi, together with tourists and pilgrims from all the corners of the world. In this day and age of secularisation it is interesting to see that the old tradition of making a pilgrimage is still sustained and even increasingly popular – Santiago de Compostela, Taizé, Iona, Assisi; modern-day humanity longs for an old and a new link between heaven and earth.

In Luke's Gospel, for a moment, heaven comes to earth. Unexpected, unannounced: it just happens to the people there; they have no choice – and at first it frightens them! The shepherds in the fields are social outcasts, but they have been chosen by God: His glory is all around them. The good news for everyone is first heralded to people who have no status in life, the nobodies. The words spoken and the songs sung are of vital importance. They are full of meaning, a dangerous meaning, a political meaning even. The message sounds like the proclamation of a victory, or the crowning of a new king. The titles Messiah and Lord were usually restricted to great rulers and conquering heroes. The words 'honour' and 'peace' were traditionally used by the masses to greet their war heroes at their glorious entry. These words are used here for a reason. What Luke wants to say is: this child is the anti-king by the grace of God. He is the One who actually holds the future of the world in his hands. He is the real champion of the underdogs and the oppressed. The David-king as opposed to Goliath-Augustus. The born Shepherd. God's policy of peace as opposed to the policy of violence and injustice. A God who identifies himself with ordinary people, instead of a god throwing his weight around.

In the bookshop of the basilica, a card on one of the shelves catches my eye: 'Our Lady with the Child'. A picture of a fresco in the Church of St Clare, a bit further on the road. There is Mary with the child, with golden 'pancakes' around their heads, the oxen and the donkey watching merrily, in loving adoration.

Mostly, however, I am moved by the pair of outstretched hands in the bottom right-corner of the picture, reaching out to the child. Why these outstretched hands, and whose hands are they? ...

Suddenly for me this old fresco, such a well known icon of our culture, turns the gospel into a verb of action. Christmas is not a matter of 'once upon a time', a famous image. Christmas is a matter of then, now and tomorrow.

God came down to earth in human form as Jesus and in doing so entered into our world and into our humanity. He broke, and is still breaking, into our world. Christmas stirred and is still stirring into motion all relationships, also our own, that at first seemed immovable and beyond repair. Heaven and earth are again interconnected in this child. It is not just a friendly act of God, but an act born out of disappointment and despair towards people who have lost their sense of destiny. He wants to restore his hopes for us and strengthen our faith in him. It is a cause for celebration because our human fear of insignificance, exploitation and oppression has been dispelled. This is something to reach out for, to receive and share.

In the Church of St Clare, I search for the fresco reproduced on the card: whose hands are they? ... There they are, mother and child and the outstretched hands …

Do we know who these hands belong to? Do we know who reaches out for our hands?

Prayer

God, we thank you for the feast of Your coming into the world in this child. Your hands, reaching out to people, then, now and tomorrow. You said, 'Do not be afraid, accept my love, live and share it with others.' May we be focussed on this love, receive it and share it.

May our hands be a blessing to those around us, all people – refugees, strangers and all those who feel alienated, lost and lonely at Christmas. Amen

Teun Kruijswijk Jansen, translated by Elisabeth van Aller

Teun Kruijswijk Jansen is a Reverend of the Protestant Church in the Netherlands and is specialised in spiritual accompaniment. He is a member of the Iona Community and one of the founders of the Dutch Iona group: www.ionagroep.nl/

December 14

Luke 2:10–11

Not an opera god

A saviour is born! This is good news indeed. How often I have prayed for a God who comes to save, to help, to turn the tide of the inevitable. A God like those gods of baroque opera, who descend to earth to disentangle the mess of human life. When we despair, we pray for a 'God of happy endings'. We want to experience God's goodness here and now and immediately. When my daughter-in-law was dying of cancer, I prayed for a miracle against all medical evidence. Against all hope, I hoped for a saviour who would wave his magic wand so that all manner of things would be well.

It didn't work that way. And yet, the childhood wish 'come, help, save' is often on my lips. Come and drive my fear away, my doubts, my very real powerlessness in the face of forces much larger than me.

The message of the angels that a saviour is born responds to our deepest need to be saved, to be 'delivered from evil', to be freed from the assault of illness and death, from the mystery of unanswered love, from the violence that human beings inflict on each other; and also from the greed and stubbornness of our hearts and our moral cowardice. But the angels of the biblical Christmas story do not announce the entry of an opera god. They speak of the birth of a child. The saviour they proclaim is a newborn infant who has to be nurtured and teased into life. A saviour who has yet to train for the toilet and to bubble his first words. Who has to learn to walk into the world, to stumble and fall and get bruises and to have someone hold him by the hand and sing – in whatever language – the old healing chant 'Heile, heile Segen' when it hurts. A saviour who is totally dependent on the care of parents, family and friends. Who needs to experience a peace-filled and sharing community in order to trust that peace with justice could be the alternative to the rat race of greed, violence and profit-making that crushes so many people and destroys the earth.

The saviour born this day is forever in the state of becoming.

Later, at around age 30, after having lived a full life, he will walk into the world and proclaim that the kingdom of God is near. Not there yet, but near. And so again all those who hear the message are begged to make it come true, to participate in the mystery of becoming 'saviours' themselves.

To be able to do that we have to feel our way into discerning the message. Those men and women, guarding their flock in the fields of Bethlehem, were able to do that. Other folk in Bethlehem were probably asleep in their beds, or occupied with chores or pleasures, or maybe too worried, too careless or too happy to hear anything. Let alone the politicians and businessmen of Jerusalem, so concerned about their power and safety and how to keep both.

It is not easy to discern the 'powerless God' of peace in our midst. The God who has entrusted Godself to a fragile baby born in a shelter in Bethlehem; to a woman suffering the loss of mental and physical control of Alzheimer's; to a soldier before he pulls the trigger; to a hungry young mother in a *favela* in Salvador de Bahia; to a speechless, yearning youngster who drinks himself into a coma on a school ground in Zürich …

It is not easy to see God's image in all of these. And often it is not easy to see

God's image in ourselves. Because we can be both 'the portrayer and the prison for Christ's intention for man', we pray, with a meek heart: 'Take, O take me as I am; summon out what I shall be.' The saviour in you and me will grow with every small act born out of respect for the dignity of people and creation, with all our efforts to love and to protect life, with every little sign of peace. These may not win the day. But it is important to do them, together, and in this way to 'do' God in this world. Not all tides will be turned in this way, not all mysteries of suffering will be solved; but our lives and the lives of others will be more healed and beautiful!

Prayer

All-loving God, in the hustle and noise of our lives
help us to hear your voice
in the voices of all who yearn and struggle for peace
and who suffer the pangs of a new earth being born,
where justice will reign. Amen

Reinhild Traitler-Espiritu

Reinhild Traitler-Espiritu is an educator and theologian, who worked for many years with the World Council of Churches. Until her retirement in 2003, she was Director of Programme at the Protestant Academy Boldern, Zürich, with a portfolio on feminist theology and interreligious learning. She is currently co-directing the European Project for Interreligious Learning (EPIL) and serves on the Interreligious Thinktank, Switzerland. Her latest book is Es Muss Nicht Der Siebte Himmel Sein *(It Does Not Have To Be Cloud Nine), 2009. She is a member of the Iona Community.*

December 15

Luke 2:10–11

An Iona Christmas

> *'Only a demanding common task builds community.'*
> George MacLeod, Founder of the Iona Community

There's a 'house party' on Iona at Christmastime. Volunteers come from all over the world to welcome guests, some of whom have been going through very tough times all year.

I remember a party we had once in the Abbey common room at the end of one of those weeks, following a Communion service in the Michael Chapel. It was like the whole world was in that room – folk from America, Poland, Wales, Pakistan …

Charles was talking to Stuart. Charles was from Hampstead Heath in London and Stuart was from Possilpark in Glasgow. Stuart had needed to get clear of where he was staying for a bit – had needed to get away from the temptation of drugs and drink. Stuart and Charles had seemed worlds apart. They'd barely understood each other's accents at first, and could hardly carry on a conversation around the table at mealtimes.

Joan was playing Christmas carols on her acoustic guitar – and TJ was singing. Joan described herself as 'a radical feminist singer-songwriter'; TJ played American football. He had a surprisingly soft and gentle voice; subtle phrasing. There'd been some ups and downs in the week (as usual) and at one point TJ and Joan had shouted and screamed at each other in the middle of community chores. Now they were sitting making music:

> *'It came upon the midnight clear,*
> *that glorious song of old,*
> *from angels bending near the earth*
> *to touch their harps of gold ...'*

In many ways it was like the end of any typical week on Iona.

Pauline and Maggie were talking to Sofija and Pristina, who were volunteers. Pauline and Maggie were sisters. Their ninety-three-year-old mother had died in September and they'd come to Iona for Christmas because they had used to come to Iona with their father and mother when they were girls. It was a place they both loved and had felt happy. Something they had in common. I glanced round the common room. Stuart and Charles were exchanging addresses now. Later, I saw the sisters sitting together in the cloisters, watching the first snowflakes fall, clouds of their breath and cigarette smoke mingling in the air.

'Thanks. I've never *had* a good Christmas,' Stuart said to me going out of the common room, and into the night.

> *'... when peace shall over all the earth*
> *its ancient splendours fling,*
> *and all the world give back the song*
> *which now the angels sing ...'*

I went outside, in back of the Abbey; there was moonlight on the sea and I gazed up at the stars. I could see an announcement in the sky: It said that the whole world could be reconciled: brothers from Possil and Hampstead Heath, women and men, neighbours from Serbia and Kosovo, estranged sisters ... The world had travelled to the 'world island' of Iona to come together and be touched and healed. And the Earth is an island in the sea of the universe, I thought. A common room in God's many-roomed mansion. And I closed my eyes and breathed in the stars and earthy night ...

When I left Iona I took that announcement back. It's harder to see the stars on the mainland, with the pollution, interference, glare ... Sometimes I walk out to the country-dark to remember that night. Sometimes I need to come all the way back to Iona to be reminded of infinite possibilities.

> There is no rich or poor,
> no male or female:
> All are one in Jesus Christ.
>
> No black or white,
> no First World or Third World:
> All are one in Jesus Christ.
>
> No 'radical feminist singer-songwriter',
> no conservative American football player:
> All are one in Jesus Christ.
>
> No ex-junkie living in a park,
> no cocaine addict wandering lost on a heath:
> All are one in Jesus Christ ...
>
> *Turn off your TV screen that breeds fear*
> *and go outside*

and gaze up at the awesome sky
full of promise …

Breathe in the stars
smell the night
Christ is born today and every day …

Neil Paynter

Neil Paynter was a member of the Iona Community's Resident Group on Iona from 1997–2001. He is the Editor of Coracle: the magazine of the Iona Community, *an editor with* Wild Goose Publications, *and the author of* Down to Earth: Stories and Sketches (Wild Goose).

December 16

Luke 2:10–11

Places of salvation around the world: Corrymeela, Vellore, Iona ...

I remember my first visit to Corrymeela, one of the Iona Community's sister communities in Ireland, which works for peace and reconciliation. As I left the building I saw a text above the door. It read: *'Corrymeela begins when we go home.'* My mind flashed back to my early days in India and to my and my wife Anne's first visit to Vellore Christian Medical College and Hospital, where we were shown round the wards. In the Premature Baby Unit we saw a tiny baby who had been brought from a distant village by bullock cart. The wee soul had been struggling for life and but for her parents' faith and the loving care of nurses and doctors she would have died. On our way to the main door of the hospital we passed through the chapel and then out into the throbbing streets of Vellore. Above the main door we saw a text, from St Luke's Gospel. It read: *'Mine eyes have seen thy salvation'* (Luke 2:30). As we thought of that little baby and of all the other healing work which we had just witnessed we knew that that text was so very true. Our eyes had seen God's salvation.

The idea of starting a hospital occurred to Ida Sophia Scudder in the late 1800s, when Ida visited her medical missionary father, John Scudder, Jr., at his post in Tamil Nadu. One night, Ida was asked to help three women from different families struggling in difficult childbirth. Custom prevented their husbands from accepting the help of a male doctor and, being without training at that time, Ida herself could do nothing. The next morning she was shocked to learn that each of the three women had died. She believed that it was a calling and a challenge set before her by God to begin a ministry dedicated to the health needs of the people of India, particularly women and children. Consequently, Ida went back to the USA, entered medical training and, in 1899, was one of the first women graduates of the Weill Medical College of Cornell University.

Shortly thereafter, she returned to India and opened a one-bed clinic in Vellore in 1900. Two years later, she built a 40-bed hospital. In 1909, she started the School of Nursing, and in 1918, a medical school for women was opened under the name Missionary Medical School for Women. The medical school was upgraded to a university-affiliated medical college granting the degree of M.B.B.S. in 1942, under the name Christian Medical College (CMC). Men were admitted to this college in 1947, ten in a class of 35.

In addition to the medical and nursing schools that she founded, Dr Ida frequently visited outlying villages, and started a roadside dispensary of sorts, in 1916. Over the years, these roadside dispensaries were upgraded into rural health and development programmes. Today CMC hospital is a referral tertiary care hospital. CMC's graduates stay on to work in hospitals affiliated to the Christian Medical Association of India. Each year 60 students, of which at least 25 are women, are admitted for the undergraduate medical course (M.B.B.S.). Training in Community Medicine involves daily village visits to collect data about disease prevention awareness, child malnutrition, living conditions, socio-economic status and educational status. CMC is consistently ranked amongst the top three medical colleges in India, ranking second in the 2009 survey.

This Advent – as we remember Iona and our Columban heritage, Corrymeela and its continuing to be, as its name suggests, 'a hill of harmony', Vellore and so many other places of salvation around the world – we can rejoice with the angel who has brought good news of great joy for all the people. It was this same joy which enveloped the old man Simeon when, inspired by the Spirit, he recognised the Messiah in the face of a little baby in the temple at Jerusalem. When that baby became a man, he left the very same temple and sat on the Mount of Olives. There in that place of olive branches he taught his disciples to feed the hungry, to give drink to the thirsty, to welcome the stranger, to clothe the naked, to heal the sick and to visit those in prison. He then told them: *'As you do it to one of the least of these, you do it to me'* (Matthew 25:40).

If we wish to meet Jesus this Christmas and experience the good news of great joy for all people, we would do well to remember with Ray Davey of Corrymeela, George MacLeod of Iona and Ida Scudder of Vellore that our personal Corrymeela begins not on the mountaintop, but down in the valley in those places which we call home.

A prayer from India

Loving God, as we journey through Advent we know that on Christmas morning we will hear a baby cry. We know that we will see you edged out of society and into a stable to be born in poverty and great humility. Some of us wonder at it all. We are touched and we're troubled. Yet sometimes it is just another Christmas and we couldn't care less. Move us now, O God. Trouble us. Disturb us to the very depths of our being that we may so serve the hungry and thirsty, the stranger and the naked, the sick and those in prison, that this Advent may become different for us, thus enabling us to be properly prepared to receive the gift of the Christ child on Christmas Day. This we ask in Jesus' name. Amen

Murdoch MacKenzie

Murdoch MacKenzie has been a member of the Iona Community since 1965. He and his wife, Anne, worked in South India for twelve years.

www.corrymeela.org
www.cmch-vellore.edu
www.iona.org.uk

December 17

Luke 2:10–11

What have we learnt in two thousand years?

Day one

3am. The world is asleep, but inside Ben Gurion Airport it is a hive of activity. I wait for our guests to arrive, and become aware of a wide range of nationalities and languages, and the diversity of the people who come and go: striking Orthodox male Jews with amazing beards, hats and distinctive apparel; the Orthodox Jewish families with lots of children; a few Muslim families, in traditional Arab dress; next to very casually attired Western tourists. Our guests arrive – pleased to see a welcoming face.

In the afternoon, we visit a Muslim village in the West Bank countryside. An Israeli settlement built on a nearby hill is now being expanded in their direction. Kate, a young American, tells how villagers are being violently harassed by aggressive settlers. Kate is a member of a peacemaking organisation and has assisted this community every summer for the last six years. 'Why do you do this?' one of our group asks. 'Peace isn't just a word in a book,' she says. 'You have to be the peace you want to see.' A local community leader explains, 'We are farmers. Resistance for us is to continue to farm our fields. Our non-violent retaliation has brought international support and Israeli human rights organisations to help us.'

In the evening, at dinner, we meet a 'Rabbi for Human Rights' who shares his vision of a State of Israel where everyone can feel they belong, no matter their religion or ethnic background.

Our guests reflect. Why is there so much pain here, when there is such a will within parts of the community for reconciliation and peace?

Day two

An early start and it is already hot. We visit a small Israeli settlement built high in the hills in the West Bank near Hebron. We speak to a Jewish settler who invites us to his house for refreshments, and tells us about his study of the scriptures and his belief that God promised this land to his people. We ask him about the local Arab communities who have lived for generations in the valley below. He does not connect to them – all that is important are the priorities of God, and people should not stand in the way.

Our guests are disturbed. The settler truly believes that God personally promised him the land three thousand years ago, and he does not acknowledge that other people have any claim to this land.

This reminds me of an image used by George MacLeod: The flower has a beauty to share with all of us. Some of us want to own that beauty for ourselves, so we pluck it. In the process of taking it for ourselves, we remove the beauty from its source of nourishment, and it dies.

Later, we visit an organisation in East Jerusalem and share Communion with local Arab Christians. Over coffee we talk, and are given personal family stories of loss, and of being cut off from places of personal identity by barriers and the requirement for permits, rarely granted. The pain and longing is heartfelt and long-standing. People are being made to feel strangers in their own land.

In the evening we join a Jewish family for their Shabbat meal. Here we experience strong family values, share wonderful food, and liturgy holding past and present together. We gain a strong sense from this family that they are in their rightful place – even though they have only been here for ten years.

Our guests are shocked by the proliferation of weapons and physical barriers they have seen today. But they are more deeply disturbed by the conflicting narratives: one expressing a God-given right to the land; another talking about birthright and tradition; and a third based on an internationally recognised right to settle here. How can there be peace in this land, our guests ask? How can you reconcile the irreconcilable?

Day three

Today we came face-to-face with the army at a checkpoint as we came out of the West Bank on our way to Tiberias. One of our group had forgotten his passport. At first, the young soldier at the checkpoint indicated that this was a very serious matter. But then he waved us through, with a stern reminder that, as internationals, we must always carry our passports.

Later, we hear from the Bishop why he missed the interfaith meeting he was to host for us. He was delayed at the same checkpoint. All his papers were in order but still he was instructed to park and wait while they check them. An hour later his papers were returned, and he was waved on – with no explanation for the delay. He is an Arab Christian – so perhaps no other explanation was needed.

Our guests recoil at the unfairness and the misuse of power. Everything is constructed to consolidate the barriers that keep people apart.

At evening worship, the pastor considers the healing in Luke's Gospel that takes place on the east side of the Sea of Galilee – in the land of the Gerasenes. A story replete with images – of a demonised man who haunts the tombs, and the herd of pigs that rush to their deaths in the lake.

Every player has something to fear in the story: the demonised man in his isolation; the demons in their recognition of Christ; the community who cannot deal with the evil in their presence, or cope with change. And there is also fear amongst the disciples themselves – good Jewish seekers after truth, but outside their comfort zone. The scripture suggests that Jesus chose to bring his group here – to walk into this fearful and alien environment and bring healing and wholeness.

Our guests are deeply struck by worshipping close to where this incident happened. One points out that there are different forces operating today, but fear is still pervasive. What have we learnt in two thousand years? Why are we still so afraid of people who are different from us and have different beliefs?

People here need to feel the reconciling presence of God as much now as they did two thousand years ago.

'Do not be afraid,' said the angel.

Prayer

Lord God, you chose your time and place to act in human history.

You chose a place with many barriers and boundaries, where people were struggling with identity, where the exercise of power had created many divisions.

You chose to begin by sharing the good news of wholeness and reconciliation with broken, wounded people.

We are wounded still. We fear the costs of reconciliation. Help us to not be afraid of you, or each other. Help us to find our true humanity, our sense of who we are, in your mercy and in your graciousness.

George Shand and Margaret Pressland

George Shand and Margaret Pressland live in Jerusalem. George is the Church of Scotland minister of St Andrew's Scots Memorial Church in Jerusalem. Prior to this he was a minister in Leith (near Edinburgh). He has a history of working in international fair trade, and disability and employment. Margaret has worked in community health and community economic development in marginalised communities in Scotland. Between them they have three children. George Shand is an Associate member of the Iona Community.

December 18

Luke 2:10–11

Tying justice onto the tanabata tree: Words from Japan

The shepherds heard it. What did they think? They were amongst the poorest people in first-century Palestine. What would have been good news to them?

Early first-century Palestine was a time of change. Taxes by the Romans, taxes by Herod for his massive building projects, were driving the Palestinian people into poverty. A failed harvest meant being in debt or driven from the family's land. There must have been fear of poverty and destitution and uncertainty among the people. What could have brought them great joy, but news that the oppression from Roman and Jew alike was ended; that they would be allowed to live their lives and farm their land in peace.

The Romans, of course, insisted that it was a time of peace, the Pax Romana. They cracked down on vagrants and bandits and made the roads safe for travel and trade. The peace was peace for the wealthy, protecting wealth first, people second and the poor and their possessions by accident, if at all.

Here in Japan, peace is a word whose fortune I regularly follow. In Japanese, the word is *heiwa* and is made up of two *kanji* characters. The first, *hei*, means 'level, peaceful, just', the second, *wa*, means 'peace, harmony and unity'. *Wa* is also used to mean Japanese: *wafu* means 'in the Japanese way', *washoku* means 'Japanese food'. The Japanese people have identified themselves for centuries as a people of peace.

It is easy to see why. I have been to Hiroshima for the anniversary of the nuclear attack and it strikes me that the response to such an atrocity has not been one of revenge or resentment but a plea that it should never happen again. I have marched to protest against planned changes to Article 9 of the Japanese Constitution, a clause that insists that Japan will not arm or use weapons against another country. (And though it seems to me that Japanese people are, in general, politically apathetic, on this topic they are not.) And during the *tanabata* festival in July, when we write our wishes on coloured paper and tie them to bamboo trees in our local parks, I enjoy seeing the word HEIWA next to my own multi-coloured English PEACE.

There is a feeling of peace and safety here. I live in Tokyo, but leave my door and windows open when I go to the shop. I have never seen road rage. I walk by young people, even teenagers, without fear of harassment. And when I return to Scotland on holiday, I feel an underlying tension that I am in a place where peace, balance, harmony, *wa* is not important.

But what kind of peace is it that I live in? Is it a Roman peace, a peace protecting only those who have; or is it a peace which also looks out for those who have not? Japan's peace is, I believe, based on its equality. Something like 95% of Japanese people see themselves as middle class, over 99% can read (one of the highest literacy rates in the world). Sometimes this equality appears to be, and maybe is, a lack of individuality, a sameness. It's not that there isn't poverty here but, compared to Britain, it feels like money and opportunities are more evenly spread.

So is it a Pax Romana with a difference, where those who are well-off are protected, but since almost everyone has money or opportunity, almost everyone is protected? What about the 5% who do not see themselves as middle class or as fitting into the Japanese norm? Do they need to be protected from Japan's Roman peace?

I think they do. Because there is a lot of sameness here, being different has its issues. Discrimination against foreigners, especially Asian or African foreigners, discrimination against women and low investment in special education are some of the injustices I have come across in my life here.

I begin to wonder: Should I really be wishing and praying so much for peace? Looking around, what is lacking in my society is a strong sense of justice. A sense that if something isn't fair it needs to be changed, no matter how much that would disturb the peace. And here, although the peace movement is big and influential, awareness of movements centred around justice, such as the fair trade movement and movements to addresss world poverty, are weak.

So the good news that my society needs may be less one of peace and more one of disturbance. Maybe next July, as well as a big colourful PEACE, I'll write a big colourful JUSTICE to tie on the *tanabata* tree.

Prayer

What does the world around us ask of us?
What great joy can we bring to it?
Give us understanding of where we are,

of how to respond to the darkness and light of what is around us.

Give us your peace that is born of, and inextricable from, your justice.
Help us to tie it into our lives and work, even if it means
upsetting and unsettling everything and everyone around us. Amen

Alison Gray

Alison Gray is from Scotland but has lived for the past eleven years in West Tokyo. She lives in a messy old Japanese house with her son. She writes, edits and teaches. She is an Associate member of the Iona Community.

December 19

Luke 2:10–11

A Kairos moment

In October 2009 I stayed with a Palestinian family in Beit Sahour, the Shepherds' Fields area in the city of Bethlehem. I was part of a group of thirty-four internationals from all over the world who had come to Palestine/Israel to assist with the annual olive harvest. Not that Palestinian farmers need help to harvest their olives; our presence is an act of solidarity and support in their struggle to retain their land in the face of the encroachment of the separation barrier and the inexorable expansion of Israeli settlements. Beit Sahour means literally 'the house of not sleeping'! On the night shift the shepherds dare not sleep. They are guardians of the flock against attacks by marauders and wild animals.

Some months after I left Beit Sahour, the local people were peacefully demonstrating against the decision of the Israeli Defence Force to take over land 'for security purposes' – land which had been designated for a much-needed community recreational area. Here, another kind of vigilance and wakefulness is necessary.

Today many men in Bethlehem hardly sleep. If you visit the approach to the huge Gilo checkpoint or terminal any time between 2am and 6am you will find hundreds of men with a smaller number of women queuing to pass through to workplaces in and around Jerusalem, less than seven miles away. Every morning – except Saturdays – all the year round, and in all weathers. This, too, is apparently for security purposes.

Just down the road, Aida Refugee Camp (one of several in Bethlehem), occupying an area of 1.5 square kilometres, is home to 21,000 souls, many of them children and teenagers. Here people sleep fitfully. It is not a silent place. When helicopter gunships fly overhead and sonic booms are heard in the night, sleep is disturbed. A father tells me of his little girl, who, since the second intifada in 2002 (when the Israeli military laid siege to the Church of the Nativity and homes were raided after midnight), still sometimes wakes up terrified, and regularly wets her bed. Fear stalks the streets of modern Bethlehem. Do we think of this when we sing our carols?

On Sunday, Hanna meets me outside the Church of the Nativity. He is an Orthodox Christian and well known on Iona, where he has worked as a volunteer. We go to his home to meet his wife and family and share a meal together. Afterwards he takes me up to the roof of the house, which commands a superb view of Bethlehem and the area beyond Jerusalem towards Jericho and the Dead Sea. We see the monstrous wall, effectively imprisoning the people of the city; he points to the nearby hillside dominated by the grey-stone Israeli settlement of Har Homa, illegally built over an area of outstanding natural beauty, slowly moving down the slopes of the hill towards the city, eating up yet more Palestinian land.

Once again the truth dawns: Bethlehem today is a community under Occupation, just as it was in the time of Jesus. This Occupation has lasted for 43 years and shows no sign of coming to an end. The word first heard by the shepherds of Beit Sahour was addressed to an oppressed people longing for freedom from the rule of Rome's Empire. It was embodied in the man whose message was gloriously inclusive – news of great joy for ALL people!

Many in our world are asleep. They speak of peace when there is no peace.

Just before Christmas last year, a group of Christian leaders met in Bethlehem to launch a document called *A Moment of Truth: A Word of Faith, Hope and Love from the Heart of Palestinian Suffering.** It has become known as Kairos Palestine – a wake-up call to Christians and all people of goodwill around the world to stand in solidarity with our Palestinian sisters and brothers in their time of crisis.

We are the modern angels – messengers called to speak and embody this urgent word of justice, peace and hope alongside Palestinians and Israelis, where hatred, greed and fear combine to oppress and to separate. In the words of Alice Walker: '*We are the ones we have been waiting for.*'

Prayer

Living, loving God, as we listen again to the cry of your people in the land where Jesus was born, may we truly hear that cry – and then be silent no longer, joining our words and our deeds with those who insist that there can be no peace without justice and are already making a difference.

In the Name of the great Liberator, child of Bethlehem, man of Galilee, crucified and risen in Jerusalem, let loose in all the world. Amen

Warren R. Bardsley

Warren R. Bardsley: 'I am a Lancastrian trained in Manchester for the Methodist ministry, who spent the next 40-odd years travelling in West Africa and in a variety of English circuits, both urban and rural. I joined the Iona Community (Associate 1995, full member 2007) after working with my wife as a volunteer on Iona in 1993. I became passionate about the Palestinian cause following a visit to the country in 2005 with the Amos Trust, and subsequently served as an Ecumenical Accompanier in East Jerusalem.' (www.eappi.org)

*Available from Friends of Sabeel UK, CMS, Watlington Road, Oxford OX4 6BZ
Sabeel is a grassroots liberation theology centre in Jerusalem. 'Sabeel works for a just peace for the people of Palestine and Israel. Started by Palestinian Christians, Sabeel promotes non-violence and reconciliation.'
(From the Sabeel UK website: www.friendsofsabeel.org.uk)

December 20

Luke 2:10–11

In my early twenties it felt to me that Canada (where I lived at the time, and was born) was becoming more and more bland and Americanised – and I felt a desperate need to escape the soulless monoculture before it was too late, and to see the world.

I kept a journal while travelling. Following are a couple extracts from that journal: one from when I was in Africa; and another from when I was travelling through Yugoslavia, not long before its break-up and the bloody Balkan wars.

Waiting for the light (Benin, West Africa)

… Vendors rush up to us as we're idling in the Land Rover. Waiting for the light at congested, confused intersections – bush taxis; mini-buses; rattling pick-up trucks; someone pushing a wheelbarrow; someone pulling a cart; mopeds; motorbikes; a Mercedes; a goat … Rush up to us – selling necklaces made of cowrie shells, *gri-gri* charms, newspapers – *Echos D'Africa*: 'The Carnage of Rwanda', *Le Forum*: 'The Devaluation of the CFA – How Will We Cope?' – disposable razors, a clothes iron reflecting searing sun, a kitchen knife set, tubes of Crazy Glue, plastic baggies of some kind of white powder (not cocaine, but rat/cockroach poison), tubes of Close-up toothpaste, Chiclets, a short-wave radio, a manicure set, a set of plastic bowls – a surreal variety for *Yovos* and African elites: the African home shopping network; your screen a half-rolled-down window. A 'Tummy Trimmer'. It's pretty depressing seeing someone malnourished trying to sell exercise equipment. 'C'est bon pour vous, Madame', a smiling maybe eight-year-old boy schooled in pitches calls to my girlfriend, sitting in the back-seat of the Land Rover; on the battered cardboard box, a sun-faded photo of a smiling first-world blonde, sitting on her living room carpet, rowing in her Tummy Trimmer. 'C'est très bon pour vos santé,' he pitches again. 'No, mais merci.' We smile regretfully; stare straight ahead … An old woman being led by a little girl. The old woman blind, chanting something in *Fon*, hand held out. Eyes whited out by Oncho. Onchocerciasis. River Blindness. Hell, no change. 'Any change in your bag, dear?' The traffic moves on. 'Prochain fois, Madame, Mademoiselle!' we call. 'Next time.' And our exhaust blots them out … Next:

A woman with a look of impassive dignity selling pink toilet paper, the rolls piled on a tray balanced on her head.

A man selling shoes, two pair in one hand and three in the other, his fingers all splayed out, painfully. He walks around the city all day in his thick-skinned bare feet selling hard men's shoes … Next light: a girl of three or four selling oranges and boxes of wooden matches – the cars and motor-bikes and trucks screeching and snorting all around her – such a tiny, frag-ile being, wading through all that danger, a heavy basket of fruit balanced on her thin neck.

A young boy runs up to the window. I don't understand his French accent, so he tries again in English: 'Want to buy a house?' he says. 'A house?' I repeat, feeling guilty, wealthy. 'No, not *house*,' he pronounces, tired, and desperate underneath. '*Horse. Cheval.*' 'Oh, horse, horse,' I laugh. 'No, sorry, sorry.' We drive on. And I think of all those sentimental, first-world boy-and-his-horse stories, and have a sudden vision of a horse with its hip bones protruding; its chest ribbed like rusty corrugated roofing.

Since the devaluation of the CFA, our driver tells us, people are so desperate they'll do anything for money. Two of a gang of thieves were lately caught, he says, and dragged down to the beach, and chained to poles. As they were being stoned, some other people stood around taking photos. To sell. And we drive on, leaving a crowd of children, women, men, waiting for the light …

Prayer

Jesus Christ,
forgive us for all the ways we tell you 'Next time'
and pass you by
while you are standing
waiting for the light …

The waiting room (Zagreb, Yugoslavia)

… Downtown: posh as Geneva. Sparkling as mineral water. Women wrapped in furs. Men armoured in suits. Teenagers standing eating hamburgers, getting ketchup on their football jerseys.

I take a tram away out to the suburbs. First, neighbourhoods of huddled houses. Further out, everyone crammed into grey apartment buildings. I don't know how many in one room. On every balcony clothes hanging. Like pieces of dead skin flapping in the grimy wind. No parks or grass out here, no connection to the earth. Most everyone living in mid-air.

Zagreb train station: Drunk men wandering in and out, yelling at me, yelling at God.

In the long, narrow waiting room, one long line of hard, black, bolted-down chairs in which few passengers sit. It's more a waiting room for the discarded souls from the street, and they're waiting to die.

It's packed: An old woman with swollen arms and legs, patches of running sores – dented head hanging down between her quivering legs, a puddle of piss underneath her chair. I cautiously wake her. Offer her bread and cheese. She takes it, cautiously. A few minutes later, timidly asks me for a 'cig'. (I don't smoke.) *'Vala'* (thank you), she squeaks, finishing her bread and cheese and immediately burrowing her head back down between her legs. As if, after so many years of being invisible, she has turned into a hole.

A young man beside me with a bandaged hand, bandage unravelling, wound dirty. It looks infected. Smells infected. He wants to talk; have a conversation. But we can't talk together. He wants a cigarette. (I don't smoke.) I point to his hand. 'O-K?' 'English O-K,' he replies. 'Yugoslavia, *nein* O-K.' And he turns away, still lonely, still craving.

My train leaves at 11.00pm. It's only 7.30. A gypsy woman wants *dinars*. I give her little child cheese. Wants *dinars*. Won't leave me be. I get up and walk away. They follow me. I walk faster-faster. She follows fast-faster. She tugs on my coat. I turn around, and throw her a savage look. She ducks, retreating. Leaves me alone.

Her child throws my cheese away. On each of my anxious rounds of the pulsing station, I pass it, lying on the scuffed floor. Soon it's smushed by a heavy boot. By the third hour, marching insects have come to claim it.

I get on my train at 11:00pm and leave the discarded crowd, waiting for death to pull up. Or for the police to come, and give them a hard kick, and chase them out into the cold, infinite void of night.

Prayer

God, forgive us for pursuing the American dream –
for standing eating hamburgers
and getting ketchup on our designer jerseys –
while brothers and sisters
dumped in the waiting rooms of the world
                   sit
waiting to die.

Forgive us for the way we use our precious freedom:
travelling to endless destinations,
gazing at the shiny surface of things,
searching for all the adventure we believe is our birthright,
running away from ourselves while
chasing our dreams
(protected and insulated by money)
as your Kingdom recedes like

all the sisters and brothers
we've left behind …

O Jesus, may your birth bring an end to all this waiting –
waiting to do something meaningful with our one precious life.
Waiting for change and deliverance.

Jesus, fill us with courage.
Fill us with hope …

Neil Paynter

Before becoming an editor, Neil Paynter worked as a nurse's aide, as a 'counsellor' with people with mental health challenges, and as a night shelter worker in homeless shelters in Canada and the UK.

December 21

Luke 2:10–11

In the star-sharp stillness: Words from Ireland

How do we sing a song of the Lord in a land of plenty?

How are we, the people of Christ's Incarnation, the travelling people of God, enjoying life to its fullness? After the hard years, came the brief years of plenty, and now they are gone. Some enjoyed the years of the Celtic Tiger and some saw only the Tiger's tail. There was the party to which not all were invited, and now we are called to help with the hangover and support those who only got as far as the door.

'Dia do bheatha, idir bó agus asal' … 'Welcome, God's life to you, between ox and ass', says the traditional folk prayer.

How is God's message to change us and our world to be worked out here in the wild, wet west of Ireland, where the recession hits hard but where helping the neighbour in need is ingrained, where there is enough to eat and some money left over to enjoy the good things, where we do not hide grief though we might neglect loneliness, where government is functional though power has been corrupted, and where personal freedom is still respected but technology calls us to ever blander pleasures?

Where words of great joy are spoken each year but the kingdom has not yet come.

Behind us is the shadow, the Great Famine, which we have come to honour with the best memorial: giving to others in need across the world. Can we keep the hunger for justice in our comforted souls? As we turn again to expect mass emigration, can we act justly towards the immigrants of the fat years, those who depend on jobs so they can send overseas the money so desperately needed in their home countries, doing what we did for so long? Can we offer them, bound by economic necessity to stay, respect and support? What do we say to the children of the present, facing a rough adulthood in a land where you cannot eat the scenery, without work to make their way, and perhaps without the white light at the back of the mind to guide them? Or to those pushed beyond their strength by massive mortgages on homes they cannot heat? How do we respond as we uncover the consequences of the famine in the soul that grew out of tragedy, the small-mindedness and social control that spiralled out of control into organised brutality in the church institutions? How do we find the rich vein of great joy when we live with the legacy of the violence that formed the two States on the island?

How can we in our plenty, even with clipped wings, be the fearless bringers of great joy this year and every year? Can we be God's messengers so that the Lord of the harvest enters our lives when we let him, in good times and bad, in the cushioned recession of this decade, and in journeying with the stranger?

On Christmas night many of us still light the candle in the window and leave the door unlocked. We have done so since the times when a candle was a luxury, and a danger when left untended. Our wealth is poured out like oil this night to guide the visitor who might be a hungry tramp with a child in her arms. An anonymous poet sang in Irish eight centuries ago:

Oh king of stars!
Whether my house be dark or bright,
Never shall it be closed against anyone
Lest Christ close his house against me.

Last Christmas was the coldest for a hundred years. Waiting alone in a church at the edge of a silent town and still airport, it seemed that no one would come to worship that midnight. But in the star-sharp stillness, along ice that muffled the sound of their driving, sixteen people came to pray for the world. With our musician snowed-in at home, we had prepared tapes, but the technology froze in the cold and we sang unaccompanied, our feet beating out the rhythm to keep the blood moving, as our breath formed clouds around each head. Irish, African and English, we prayed there to the humble God who does not forget us when the pleasures of wealth make us avoid Jesus, who is there where the grief of loss and the pain of addiction hurt as deeply with the comfortable as with the poor, and who stays with us through the long recovery from the years of excess. We prayed to the God who guards those far away and those nearby on what can be the loneliest night of the year.

Seven centuries ago, another Irish poet, a learned layman, wrote in Latin:

Bestow this day on us the grace
So blithely in the joy of God to live
That those who hurt us, we this day forgive.

We started by dedicating the tree that had stood in the town centre that Advent; its branches covered with prayers written on the backs of old

Christmas cards. The tree had been by a kiosk which the recession allowed us to have rent-free, two doors down from the dominating music of Santa's grotto. An artist with her carpenter husband had designed it, and children hung angels around it, reminding us of the One who hung on a tree that embraced our prayers and sheltered our wounds. A school had lent books, and parents gave time to read to the children who flocked to the 'Room for Christmas'. A religious sister, battered from learning how her Order had abused children in its care, brought a lantern for the door. Non-nationals far from home wrote their prayers in their mother-tongues. And some came to sit on a chair in the quietest corner, which embraced stillness like a cave.

After the dedication, came the Communion, the sharing of God's bounty and life in the most silent and holy night.

Christmas morning was even colder. No one came. But other churches carried on the prayer in the town, in the county and country, and beyond across the world, with which we have such strong communion.

From four centuries ago, and in the late medieval English of Wexford, comes one of the best-loved Irish carols:

The darkest midnight in December
No snow nor hail nor winter storm
Shall hinder us for to remember
The babe that on this night was born ...

God grant us grace in all our days
A merry Christmas and a happy end.

Somehow, down the centuries, in hard times as well as in the times of peace, people have managed to sing the song of the Lord in this land, to share the good things of wealth, food, companionship, and to incorporate the stranger who follows the candlelight to knock at the door. The grace has been renewed each generation. In the words of another of the Wexford carols:

Then let us with those three kings bring
Our gifts unto this newborn King;
Our sense, our will, our wit, our heart,
And all that e'er we can impart;
Our gold, our myrrh, our frankincense,
For to adore the newborn Prince.

Rosemary Power

Rosemary Power lives in the west of Ireland and works as a Pioneer minister. She is the author of The Celtic Quest: A Contemporary Spirituality *(Columba Press) and is a member of the Iona Community.*

December 22

Luke 2:10–11

The light from the open door: Christmas in a Taiwanese village

I drove my little car along the Pacific Ocean in southwest Taiwan. It was Christmas week and I was headed to worship in one of the homes of the aboriginal Christians. The aboriginals are the native Taiwanese and have been on the island for as long as 10,000 years. Seventy percent of aboriginal people are Christian.

I turned off onto the road leading into the village and, after a number of wrong turns winding up into the mountains, finally found the home. The home was set high in the mountains off by itself. The light from the open door was a welcome sight.

As I entered, it could easily have been a home in Appalachia in the southern U.S. The church members were sitting on small chairs and stools. They were mostly older folks with faces which told of hard lives and also of deep faith. There was a young man who had been in a motorcycle accident and had suffered brain damage. The church has cared for him since his accident. There was a little girl in the next room watching TV, who came in to hear the Christmas story.

We sang the carols with a different beat, but with no less joy and hope. And then one of the women read Luke's account of the birth of Jesus in her tribal language. I then talked about the amazing way that God chose to bring Jesus into the world: It was such a risky act. And it was also risky for the humans involved. These folks understood because they know about living on the margin of Taiwan's high-tech society.

I then opened a wonderful and unorthodox picture book of the birth of Christ and began to tell the story again. They were delighted with the pictures of angels with army boots and an increasingly large Mary. They nodded their heads as a confused Joseph listened to Mary tell him of her encounter with an angel. They would chuckle and talk among themselves as I showed the pictures around the room.

If Christ were to come this Christmas, he might just come to this small Taiwanese village. It is a place that most folks don't even know exists. Christ might come to these humble aboriginal folks who would give him a wonderful welcome.

It was my privilege to be with them. After we prayed together for their children off in Taiwan's cities, working in construction or in factories, they brought out a plate laden with fresh fruit. In their faces, I saw Christ more clearly. In their mountain home I experienced the reality of the good news of great joy for all the people.

Prayer

Thank you, God, for the simple way you enter our world and our lives. Thank you for folks in our lives who are Christ to us. Amen

John McCall

John McCall spent thirteen years as a mission co-worker with the Presbyterian Church in Taiwan. He taught at Taiwan Seminary in the areas of spiritual formation and practical theology and also worked closely with the aboriginal people of Taiwan. John is currently serving as pastor of Westminster Presbyterian Church in Greensboro, North Carolina, USA. He is an Associate member of the Iona Community.

December 23

Luke 2:10–11

God breaks through the 'normal': Words from Cuba

We love to have everything under our control. We like to have everything so organised. We want to feel safe and quiet …

And when something or someone gives us challenges, we feel fear because that brings change and change means we must turn over our personal world, and we really don't like that. It is better that life runs on every day in the same way, which is many times our way.

A group of common people is working as usual. They are doing their normal activities in a normal time, in a normal way. They have organised their time as usual, to do the same things every day. But someone unknown tells them something new and brings change.

An angel broke through all that 'normal' life to say something rare and different. Something happened in life. Something that was out of human control. A Saviour was born. Why did they need a Saviour if they were living normally? Did they really need that?

God broke through history to tell these people that 'the old things have passed away: all is new from this moment', and life has to be lived in new ways every day.

Many times we are so sure that we are living in the right way; for us our traditions, business, jobs, thoughts, organisations are normal. All things are conducted in the right way, all is running in the right way; nothing has to change because we have prepared the whole of life in the right way, which is our way – a safe, easy and comfortable way. And so why do we need to change? Life runs according to our desires.

But God breaks through routine to say something new: A Saviour came and He is among us. That little child was born to break traditions, apathy, lack of sense, tired lives … God breaks 'normal things' to say new and different ones.

An angel was a messenger bringing good news from God. He is inviting us, a group of common people, to be breakers in this world like the God who sent him. An angel can be a person or a situation that gives us a message coming from God for a change in our lives.

Why do we need to change? Because our world is dying from hunger, disease, bad management of nature; because we discriminate against people who aren't in our selected group. We need a Saviour who removes from us all our sins, and show us again and again new ways to a new world.

Maybe we will feel fears, and so we need to remember the message: Don't be afraid: a Saviour is born for us.

Ask yourself: *Do I have something to change in my life? Have I rejected any angel that invited me to change? Can I be an angel to my community, family, church or country, inviting them to change? What kind of fears stop my changes?*

Prayer

Dear God, thanks because You are the One who breaks through the old. Let me know how to change things in my life and around me. Put all my fears far from me. Give me the strength to change all the things that really need to be changed. Start in my mind – and send me like an angel into this world.

Edelberto Valdés

Edelberto Valdés: 'I was born in Remedios, Villa Clara, Cuba. I am a biologist, graduated from Havana University in 1978. I worked as a lay pastor for 17 years, and I was ordained as a Presbyterian pastor on January 2nd, 2006. At this moment I am serving the Presbyterian-Reformed Church in Caibarién, Central Presbytery of the Presbyterian-Reformed Church in Cuba. I am a friend of the Iona Community.'

December 24

Luke 2:10–11

Giving up old images of ourselves: Words from Alaska

The Word comes to Alexie, native of Kwethluk, Alaska: *'You don't have to drink any more. You don't have to do drugs any more. You don't have to sleep in doorways on Fourth Avenue in Anchorage any more.'*

The Word comes to Peggy: *'You don't have to be homeless any more, couch-surfing with your children. You don't have to be afraid of your criminal history that took you from your children and left all of you homeless.'*

The Word comes to Jim and Sherry White and their sons: *'You don't have to worry about a leaking roof and mould any more.'*

It is good news to every one of them, but it is also frightening. Like for the shepherds of old on the Bethlehem hillside, the Good News engenders fear. And it is the same fear for all of them: What will my life be like when the change happens? Alexie fears he will not know how to live without a bottle or a joint. Peggy fears she won't be able to keep a job and pay the rent when she gets a new home for her family and herself. Jim and Sherry wonder if family and friends will be jealous of their good fortune. Jim, a double amputee, wonders what will keep him challenged if he no longer has to figure out how to keep fixing the roof. Sherry fears his wheelchair will mar the floor in the new house.

Change, even good change for which we have prayed often and long and hard, generates fear within us as we adapt and adjust to our new circumstances. In spite of the fear, we must embrace the change and trust that God – who thought the Big Bang and called us into being – is meeting our needs in the Servant of the Poor, Jesus, our Brother, through the invasion of the Holy Spirit as we breathe fresh air. We can enjoy the good gifts of God's love only when we are willing to give up our old images of ourselves.

Prayer

Thinker of the Big Bang of Creation; Brother Jesus who serves us with Resurrection promise; Breath of God, Holy Spirit: thank You for the good news. It is exciting. It scares us. Comfort our fear, we pray, so that we can embrace the new life You bring to us. Embrace us with understanding forgiveness when our enthusiasm is dampened by our fear of what we do not know. And then empower us to move ahead into the newness of Your promise revealed in the Babe who grows into Resurrection renewal of our lives. Amen

Israel Nelson

'I live in Wasilla, Alaska, nowhere near our half-governor, Sarah Palin. I work, part-time since my retirement in 2006, at Double Eagle Real Estate and Investments, Ltd., at Alaska Family Services Behavioral Health Center, and at Family Promise, a homeless shelter programme for children with attached parents. I am pioneering an effort to raise funds for Jim White, a double amputee who lost his legs to peripheral artery disease (www.jimalaskawhitehouse.com). I was born and grew up in Las Vegas, NV. While attending Stanford University, I became an Associate member of the Iona Community in 1966. After completing seminary and being ordained, I was pastor in three churches, and then became a substance abuse counsellor for about 40 years.'
(For information on the Iona Community in the USA, see the New World Foundation website: www.iona-nwf.org/index.html)

Christmas Eve

Luke 2:10–11

Why should I not be afraid?

'Do not be afraid!' What an introduction!

It is right in the centre of our lives – a demand and a challenge we are desperate for.

Our experiences, the news we hear, more often frighten us.

But fear is always a terrible advisor, as it paralyses us and binds our strength.

'Don't be afraid': a crisp clear first statement made by angels on Christmas Eve. You will find this demand being used, the same phrase or comparable words, 365 times in the Bible. That makes one for every day in a year. Don't be intimidated by the future; don't duck down. Whatever happens, 'Don't be afraid!'

Why should I *not* be afraid? That calls for a very good reason.

Interestingly enough, the angel himself provides the reason: great joy for all the people because of the newborn child. God came in this little child to share our life. If God shares my life, if he is interested in what I do and how I live my life – how can I be afraid?

He is there, challenging and protecting.

Prayer

God in a child,
vulnerable, ordinary – a living human.
You are my God – let me be your child,
challenged, protected, cared for, never alone;
called to serve you by serving my neighbour,
now, today, tomorrow, as long as your love is shared.

Rolf Bielefeld

Rolf Bielefeld is a member of the Iona Community who graduated in business adminis-
tration and theology. He lives with his wife, Kirsten, a deaconess of the Lutheran
Church, in Berlin, where he operates his business, a management consultancy. He is
part of the German Iona Group: www.ionacommunity.de

Christmas Day

Luke 2:10–11

**God wonderfully present, incarnate, enfleshed, in us
and all around us**

On Christmas morning 1618 in the chapel of Whitehall, London, King James VI of Scotland and James I of the United Kingdoms heard these words preached:

> *Verbum infans. The Word without a word; the Eternal Word not able to speak a word … There lieth he, the Lord of Glory without glory. Instead of a palace, a poor stable, of a cradle of state, a beast's cratch, no pillow but a lock of hay, no hangings but dust and cobwebs. For if the inn were full, the stable was not empty we may be sure.*

This is part of the sermon preached by Bishop Andrewes, one of the great preachers of his day. Andrewes loved paradox and even in that short extract you gain a sense of how he played with words:

'*The Word without a word*' – a phrase which would later inspire T.S. Eliot.

'*The Lord of Glory without glory*' – a phrase which encapsulated the theme of his sermon focussing on the poverty of the birth of Christ.

The story of the Nativity, so familiar, so sentimental to us, was for generations of believers seen as a scandal. Bishop Andrewes preached amidst the splendour of the Royal Court about the birth of the King of kings in a backward town, in a stable, in a cattle trough. Andrewes went on to explain that the nature of the birth said something about Jesus' ministry and mission and about those to whom he would proclaim the Good News.

For some the very word incarnation is a scandal. It comes from the Latin, *carno*, meaning flesh. From this root we get the English word 'carnal', of the flesh. Hence, the Incarnation speaks of the 'carnal God', the God who is enfleshed in the person of Jesus of Nazareth; literally, God *con carne*, 'God with meat on'.

Some of the great heresies of the Christian faith have been the denial of the humanity, the fleshiness, of Jesus. God, it was argued, would have nothing to do with birth and blood and flesh and filth. However, it is not the fleshiness of Christ that is the scandal for people today, it is the whole notion of God. Not only do we have difficulty believing in the Incarnation, that God became one of us, we have difficulty believing in the existence of God full stop!

Traditional Christian teaching of the Incarnation, explains that God, the Creator of all things, beyond all things, once broke into human history, in a one-off supernatural event, to be born a tiny baby to a young virgin mother.

God did this, we are told, to restore relationship with humanity and to reveal in human form truths that would otherwise be hidden.

Many, finding it impossible to believe the unbelievable, dismiss the story of the Nativity as a fairytale, and rejecting the very idea of God, find little of interest in the concept of Incarnation.

For me the Incarnation does not mean a single supernatural act but rather offers an explanation of the nature of God's relationship to the world and to all Creation. God is not seen as remote but wonderfully present, incarnate, enfleshed, in us and all around us.

The story of the Nativity tells not of a supernatural event which happened 2000 years ago in a remote corner of the Roman Empire but rather declares that the light and life and love of God was embodied in the life of Jesus of Nazareth and that this was evident even from the time of his birth. Christian belief in the Incarnation means not that Jesus, the Christ, is God-like but that God is Christ-like. The story of the Nativity invites us to make a leap of action in living a life of loving connection and engagement, acting as if God, the Divine, the Beyondness of Being, were present in everyone, in everything and in all matter.

The life and teaching of Jesus direct us towards finding God in relationship and in engagement with the world. So the shepherds are directed down from the high ground to gaze upon a baby, lying in a cattle trough, and we are directed to see God in this world as we know it, full of joy and pain, of hope and hardship, of beauty and brokenness.

The story of the Nativity convinces me to throw in my lot with God. I could not believe in any other type of God than the one revealed in the life and teaching of Jesus and that is revealed in the people and the things of this world.

Luke's story of the Nativity is not historical fact, it is a confession of faith, a declaration of belief by the first Christians. They had lived and loved as Jesus had taught them and had found his way to be true, they took that leap of action and found faith in a 'With Us' God, a God incarnate, embodied in one like them, Jesus of Nazareth.

Luke's story is then not a re-telling of a one-off, long ago event but a re-enactment of the life-long experience of God's love for the world, of God's welcome for the poor, the outcast, the stranger, and of God's invitation to us to draw near in wonder and to make that leap of action and of faith.

Peter Macdonald

Prayer

Gathered and scattered,
God is with us.
In suffering and hope,
God is with us.
Now and always,
God is with us.

A prayer from the Iona Community

Peter Macdonald is a Church of Scotland minister and the current Leader of the Iona Community.

Christmas Day reflection

'Do not be afraid; for see – I am bringing you good news of great joy for all the people: to you is born this day in the city of David a Saviour, who is the Messiah, the Lord.' (Luke 2:10–11)

Dear Reader,

Reflect on what these words from the Gospel mean to you in your present situation – on how these words speak to your daily reality and heart …

Following are a couple blank pages, if you would like to write down your reflection and prayer. Merry Christmas and Christ's Peace to you. (Eds.)

The Iona Community is:

- An ecumenical movement of men and women from different walks of life and different traditions in the Christian church
- Committed to the gospel of Jesus Christ, and to following where that leads, even into the unknown
- Engaged together, and with people of goodwill across the world, in acting, reflecting and praying for justice, peace and the integrity of creation
- Convinced that the inclusive community it seeks must be embodied in the community it practises

Together with its staff, the community is responsible for:

- The islands residential centres of Iona Abbey, the MacLeod Centre on Iona, and Camas Adventure Centre on the Ross of Mull

and in Glasgow:
- The administration of the Community
- Work with young people
- A publishing house, Wild Goose Publications
- Its association in the revitalising of worship with the Wild Goose Resource Group

The Iona Community was founded in Glasgow in 1938 by George MacLeod, minister, visionary and prophetic witness for peace, in the context of the poverty and despair of the Depression. Its original task of rebuilding the monastic ruins of Iona Abbey became a sign of hopeful rebuilding of community in Scotland and beyond. Today, it consists of about 280 Members, mostly in Britain, and 1500 Associate Members, with 1400 Friends worldwide. Together and apart, the community 'follows the light it has, and prays for more light'.

For information on the Iona Community contact:
The Iona Community, Fourth Floor, Savoy House,
140 Sauchiehall Street, Glasgow G2 3DH, UK.
Phone: 0141 332 6343
admin@iona.org.uk; www.iona.org.uk

For enquiries about visiting Iona, please contact:
Iona Abbey, Isle of Iona, Argyll PA76 6SN, UK.
Phone: 01681 700404

For books, CDs & digital downloads published by Wild Goose Publications:
www.ionabooks.com

Wild Goose Publications, the publishing house of the Iona Community established in the Celtic Christian tradition of Saint Columba, produces books, CDs and digital downloads on:

- holistic spirituality
- social justice
- political and peace issues
- healing
- innovative approaches to worship
- song in worship, including the work of the Wild Goose Resource Group
- material for meditation and reflection

For more information, please contact us at:

Wild Goose Publications
Fourth Floor, Savoy House
140 Sauchiehall Street,
Glasgow G2 3DH, UK

Tel. +44 (0)141 332 6292
Fax +44 (0)141 332 1090
e-mail: admin@ionabooks.com

or visit our website at
www.ionabooks.com
for details of all our products and online sales